Neile with best love from [illegible]

Christmas 1948.

VISION OF SCOTLAND

Barbara Jones

Crail Harbour

VISION OF SCOTLAND

BY G. S. FRASER

DRAWINGS BY BARBARA JONES

PAUL ELEK · 38 HATTON GARDEN · LONDON

Edinburgh from Calton Hill.

FOREWORD

I come of a breed of men who for centuries were the wardens of the Scottish marches, and who, as Camden the English historian records, bore the brunt of the resistance to the English invasions. Upon occasion we would be decimated to some five hundred "proper and sufficient men", but aye somehow we survived. And in my own person I represented in Parliament for over twenty years the field of Bannockburn and the Wallace monument on the Abbey Craig. So that alike by pedigree and personal contact my affinities lie in the soil north of the Cheviots, and with the folk who dwell there, and whose habits and peculiarities (or some of them) Mr. Fraser describes in the succeeding pages with such eloquence and skill.

There is a rowth of books now about Scotland and Scotsmen. For centuries prior to Scott and Burns there were few travellers reporting our mannerisms; but an Ayrshire ploughman issued from a provincial printing press a volume written "mainly in the Scottish dialect" which saved our vernacular; and Scott made our romantic history from the Orcades to the Borders known to all the English speaking world.

Since then travellers in great number have come among us: our pipe music, our kailyairds, black houses, kilted regiments, songs, dancings and theologies, have been written up, and filmed. We are on the map as a great Tourist centre and as the motherland for millions of Scots overseas. We have colonised the Empire, and now if you please we are about to colonise the homeland.

Our Councils of Industry, Hydro-Electric Boards, afforestation projects and so on, are but symptoms of an economic renaissance, an energy, a determination that Scotland shall survive as an entity in the world. Opinions may differ as to the validity of some of Mr. Fraser's generalisations. Buckle long ago pointed out the influence of soil, climate and geographical configuration upon human characteristics and habits; and no doubt but there are regional differences, obvious and marked among Scots folk. Yet while the exceptions to generalisations are many and notable William Wallace for example was active enough by all accounts, yet he came from the "feckless amiable emotional west" at any rate we are one nation now, conscious of our unity, and Mr. Fraser's "visions", attractively pictured and portrayed, make a noteworthy contribution to Scotia Resurgent.

THOMAS JOHNSTON

Home cottage. The clachan of fintry. Stirling shire.

CONTENTS

INTRODUCTION

Scotland, which is a smaller country than England - smaller in size, and disproportionately smaller in population - is also, both geographically and culturally, a less homogeneous country. Its unity is built up of striking contrasts. The contrast of which most visitors will be aware, and indeed so far as it goes it is a valid one, is that between the Highlands and the Lowlands. But this is cut across by other contrasts, of which the most important is that between the East and West Coasts. The reserve, for instance, of one traditional type of Scotsman is rather an East Coast than a Lowland characteristic; a Highlander from Helmsdale is as reserved as a Lowlander from Buchan. The expansiveness and sociability which is typical of another type of traditional Scotsman is, again, rather a West Coast characteristic than a Highland one; it is to be found as much in the Glasgow man as in the Highlander from Argyll. Here, the map of Scotland is deceptive. What is roughly true is that the West Coast has the pleasanter climate, while the East Coast has the richer soil. But the West Coast looks as if it were being savagely fretted by the sea, while the East Coast, if we make allowance for its three Firths, seems comparatively smooth. Yet it is the East Coast (on which — though Galloway, in the West, is also a fertile region — on the whole the best and most abundant arable land lies) that is bleak and bracing, while the West, even where, as in the Highlands, the soil is wretched and boggy, has a climate that is mild, damp, and relaxing. The inlets of the West Coast, the kyles and sea-lochs, are the result not so much of the sea's erosion as of the rending and crumpling of ancient rocks; and it is on the East Coast that the sea is really trying hard to bite the land away. This important climate contrast can be studied very well in Scotland's two chief cities. In Glasgow, it is supposed to be always raining, and the atmosphere certainly is damp and muggy: in Edinburgh, it is supposed to be always blowing a gale of wind along the High Street, and the visitor to Edinburgh can certainly say on most days, with the sentry in "Hamlet", that it is "a nipping and an eager air."

In Scottish history, until the Industrial Revolution, it was thus, on the whole, the East Coast with its richer soil and its more invigorating climate which set the pace. And the contrast of the feckless, amiable, emotional West and the hard, prudent, cautious East is a thread which runs through the whole Scottish story. It was in the West, with the migration of the Scots from Ireland into Argyll, that modern Scottish history began; it was from the little Western island of Iona that St Columba spread the message of Christianity among the warring Caledonian tribes. But it was in the South-East, in the Lothians, in a fragment of bleak but fertile country snatched from the Anglo-Saxon principality of Northumbria, that the Scottish kingdom was consolidated. Edinburgh, named after a North-umbrian prince, became the capital of the Celtic conquerors, and the administrative centre of the mediaeval Scottish kingdom, and it was the people of the South-East Lowlands, nearest in blood to the English (the people of the West Lowlands had a strong Brythonic strain), who proved the staunchest enemies of English ambition. The Lords of the Isles, and the North-Western clans generally, clung throughout the Middle Ages to their patriarchal organisation of society, resisted the attempts of the Stewart Kings to impose the feudal system (which, indeed, in a soil so poor as that of the Highlands would hardly have been a workable system), and were always potential allies of the English King.

The unity of the mediaeval Scottish kingdom was thus a nominal rather than a real unity. There was already a division of language, though as late as the sixteenth century probably half of the Scottish people, and not only those in the region which we now call the Highlands, spoke Gaelic. And if the Court and the South-East Lowlands generally spoke a language which they called English (still regarding Gaelic as the ancient and original Scottish tongue) that was not so much due to the greater attractiveness of English culture — as, for instance, Dr Arnold Toynbee rather naively supposes — as to the perpetual military threat which England represented, and to the frequent occupation of this region by English armies. It is a useful thing to be able to understand what an enemy is about, English was the most practically convenient language for political and military purposes in the South-East Lowlands, and the East Coast of Scotland breeds a practical strain of mind.

Thus, Scottish history, even in the Middle Ages, is generally written from the point of view of the East Lowlands; and the Highlands, with their clan fights, recede into the background. Even as early as the reign of James IV there was a tendency for a court poet like Dunbar to think of the Highlanders as a backward and barbarous people. They had managed to preserve their ancient way of life, but at the cost of losing the sympathy of the other, more practical, and more progressive section of the Scottish people. They had to defend it, as the centuries rolled by, against increasingly hostile pressure from the dominant Whig and Calvinist parties in the Lowlands, and in 1715 and 1745 they made, with astonishing vigour, their last defensive sallies. That the Gaelic language and tradition survive to-day in Scotland, and survive as something peculiarly attractive, even to the Lowlander, is something of a miracle. The Celtic element in Scottish culture may be said, from one point of view, to have been fighting a losing battle from the beginning; yet from another point of view it has survived all its defeats as something very intimately Scottish, so that even Scotsmen who speak no word of Gaelic, and who have never been out of the Lowlands, tend to feel that there is a birthright of which they have been deprived.

It is easy to take an excessively sentimental view of the Scottish Highlanders, but it is also easy, and too easy, to correct that sentimentality excessively. Dr Arnold Toynbee, for instance, in "A Study of History", compares the Highlanders to the Maoris. He regards them as a savage people, an outlying enclave of barbarism, who have at last been successfully absorbed into the main body of Western Civilisation. Whether the clearances, the depopulation of the Highlands, the scattering of a proud and ancient people to the four ends of the earth constitute a successful absorption might be doubted; but it is also true that the social and economic problems of the Highlanders who remain in Scotland are, to-day as in the reign of George III, completely unsolved. The remaining Highlanders drag out a marginal existence as fishermen, crofters, ghillies, postmen, storekeepers, and caterers for tourists; the young men are still drained abroad, or lost in great towns like Glasgow, because there is nothing for them at home. Certainly, they no longer represent a threat to "Western Civilization": but they do still cling, in spite of all sorts of official discouragement — in spite of the fact that at school, as children, they must do most of their work in English, which is a foreign language to them — to their language and traditions. They ought to be on everybody's conscience. And we can hardly expect to clear our consciences by describing this proud and ancient people, with their beautiful language, and rich culture, as savages.

One of the best answers to that claim was made, after the battle of Falkirk in 1746, by Cumberland's second-in-command, the brutal and forthright General Hawley. In justified exasperation, he circulated the following memorandum to his Intelligence Staff: "As to your diminishing their numbers, and ridiculing their discipline — you *see*, and I *feel*, the effect of it. I never saw any troops fire in platoons more regularly, make their motions and evolutions quicker, or attack with more bravery, or in better order than those Highlanders did at the battle of Falkirk. And these are the very men that you represented as a parcel of raw and undisciplined vagabonds." Such men were not savages, even though they were defending an archaic culture. But we should consider what they were defending it against. Since the seventeenth century, the Church of Scotland, dominated by East Coast Lowlanders, first by Covenanters, and then by Whigs, had been making a persistent and energetic missionary effort to destroy the ancient culture of the Highlanders and "root out their Irish language". When, towards the end of the eighteenth century, the Church of Scotland thought better of this policy, and had the Bible and the great seventeenth century Calvinist divines translated into colloquial Gaelic, its strictly religious missionary efforts had for the first time an enormous success; so that, even to-day, the Highlands of Scotland are one of the few regions in the world where High Calvinism is still a living faith. No doubt archaicism is a dangerous thing; but then Western Civilization, in Dr Toynbee's sense, is a rather abstract and general concept. If we look for Western Civilization at its most up-to-date in Scotland to-day, we find it in the shipyards but also in the dark tenements of Glasgow, and in the grim mining villages of Lanarkshire. The pleasantest things in Scotland — the life of the Border shepherds and farmers and of the East Coast fishing villages — are rather archaic. Town life, where it is pleasant, as in Aberdeen and St Andrews, and the more genteel quarters of Edinburgh, is at least rather old-fashioned. Even to-day, is not the Highlander, dragging out his wretchedly marginal existence, on the whole wise to prefer a black house in Skye to a single room in a tenement in Glasgow? Both are, in a sense, slums; but the black house in Skye is at least a slum with a beautiful background.

The life of the Scotsman in either of these places is a hard one. Scotland is, all over, a much poorer country than England. To this hardness of Scottish life, Dr Toynbee attributes the success of Scotsmen abroad, and he contrasts the typical produced by this life — "solemn, parsimonious, precise, persistent, cautious, conscientious, and well-educated" with "the traditional Englishman — frivolous, extravagant, vague, spasmodic, careless, free and easy, and ill grounded in book learning." I am not qualified to criticise Dr Toynbee's traditional Englishman; but his traditional Scotsman is, perhaps naturally enough, when we consider the South East Lowlands bias of most written Scottish history, broadly a Lowlander as contrasted with a Highlander, and more particularly an East Coast Lowlander as contrasted with a West Coast Lowlander. If we took an average Glasgow man, for instance, affable, convivial, generous, with the sort of humour that is found in the plays of James Bridie and the

The Shell Garden Leven.

speeches of Dr Walter Elliot, more interested in things than ideas, in life than in books, fond of a drink, and an enthusiast for football, we might think him almost the opposite of Dr Toynbee's figure, who resembles, rather, a certain rather old-fashioned type of Edinburgh professional man. Perhaps the history of the Scot abroad often *is* a rather dull kind of success story. The history of Scotland itself is, like the history of many Scots at home, something very different; it is rowdy, violent, humorous, coarse, poetic, dramatic, and tragic. Whatever the history of individual Scotsmen abroad may be, the history of Scotland itself is hardly a success story at all: and certainly not so in any cheap sense. "A thing that strikes me about Scottish history," writes my friend, Captain Hamish Henderson, "is the number of terse and epigrammatic phrases one finds in it, spoken and written, Gaelic and Scots. 'My Lord, your conscience clatters.' The authentic Scots spirit is realist and ironic . . . . Your kinsman Lovat taking leave of his peers that tried him: 'Farewell, my lords — we shall not meet again in one place.' Lord Balmerino surveying the London mob gathered to watch his execution on Tower Hill: 'Look how they are all piled up *like rotten oranges!*' MacDonald of Kingsburgh's comment on Prince Charlie disguised as an Irish serving maid: 'They call you a Pretender. All I can say is you're the worst at your trade I ever saw!' . . . . When Edinburgh fell, the Jacobite Army entered with such orderliness that many citizens did not know the capital had changed hands. One old burgess, finding at one point not the familiar guard but a Highland sergeant sitting non-chalantly with his broadsword across his knees, asked, 'Where's the guard?' The answer, admirably laconic, was, 'It has been changed.' . . . . Hume, stuck with his bulk in a bog, appeals for help. An old wife comes to his aid and then recognises him. 'Are *ye* no Hume the Deist?' Hume admits his identity and observes with alarm that this modern Jenny Geddes is in two minds about pulling him out. He points out that it is her *Christian* duty to do so. 'Aweel, I'll dae my Christian duty — but ye'll say the Lord's prayer first.' And say it he did . . . . MacQueen, the hanging judge, is told by a political prisoner at one of the sedition trials of the 1790's that Jesus Christ was a revolutionary. 'Aweel, what guid did that dae him? Wis he no hangit?'" One might add to that list the famous apocryphal story of the Scots Minister giving a sermon on the Last Judgment. He describes the sinners, condemned to eternal torment by God's mysterious and arbitrary election, looking up and saying, "Lord, Lord, we didna ken." "And then," said the Minister, "the Lord in his infinite mercy will look down and say to these puir sinners, 'Well, ye ken noo!'" Scottish history, Scottish life, are often violent and terrible but they never lack that style which comes, as Captain Henderson says, from the realist and ironic spirit. Nor is this epigrammatic irony, as is sometimes thought, a characteristic confined to the Lowlands: it is found, I am assured, in much Gaelic speech, and song, and poetry. From such scraps of speech, and scraps of ballad — from these fragments that convey the true life and spirit of a people — the visitor to Scotland can probably derive a truer sense of the Scottish mystery than from the dull generalisations of the historian.

Such scraps, in fact, can give one a sense of the Scottish tradition. The visitor to Scotland, however, looking for this tradition will find it most distinctively present in the less populated regions. In the agricultural Border region and in Galloway, he will be able to recreate in his imagination, as he visits the broken abbeys and the grim shells of the old keeps, the Scottish kingdom of the Middle Ages. In the Highlands and the Hebrides, he will find the small and scattered population — about four per cent of Scotland's five million — which still speaks Gaelic, Scotland's most ancient tongue; and it is there, too, that he will find the richest tradition of song and folklore. In the Orkneys and Shetlands, he will find almost pure Norse stocks. In Edinburgh, he will find the genteel tradition of Henry Mackenzie and R. L. Stevenson, in St Andrews the genteel tradition of Andrew Lang, both somewhat in decay. But in the densely populated central industrial belt, and in the hugest and most frightening city in Scotland, Glasgow, he will not be able to put his finger on any such definite tradition. He will meet, rather, as in industrial areas outside Scotland, with individuals and groups struggling to understand and control a complicated environment, whose prosperity does not depend upon local conditions; struggling to control that environment, and perhaps, if we consider slums, and unemployment, and housing shortages, and Glasgow gang-wars, largely baffled by it. The central industrial belt is not romantic or attractive. But it is where most Scotsmen live, and it is where Scotland, turning her back on the past, grapples with the future. This is the Scotland of hard fact, and it seems to be something other than the Scotland of song and story.

Glasgow, in fact, is Scotland's sadness, Scotland's problem, and Scotland's opportunity. There is a sense in which its social pattern is just a local variant of the general pattern of modern large-scale industrial civilisation; it has, as Dr Toynbee would say, been "substantially absorbed" — or horridly digested — into that pattern. Yet there is a sense also in which it is a less provincial city than Edinburgh, with its great irrelevant past, and its present painful aping of an idea of English gentility. Glasgow is alive, and alive in an unaffectedly Scottish way. It has the Scottish fury

David Glen's Bagpipe Shop,
Edinburgh.

in work, in drink, in fighting, in football matches, in politics, and in hating the smell of another man's religion; it has its Scottish pride in ships "Clyde-built". Moreover, unlike Edinburgh, it is not bowed down by the weight of the past. Its history, till the time of the industrial revolution, was a modest one. It never had much political or strategic importance. The people of Strathclyde, a Brythonic stock, emotional and impressionable, had not the political drive of the Teutonic stocks of the East Lowlands, nor the military dash of the Gaelic and Norse stocks from the Highlands. And Glasgow and the industrial belt generally are now, in any case, a melting-pot for all the Scottish races, and for many immigrant stocks, such as Southern Irish and Lithuanians, as well. Glasgow's history, at any rate, until the nineteenth century, was placid, prosperous, and undistinguished. In the seventeenth century, it had a reputation as a pleasant town, "fair, large, and well-built, cross-wise, somewhat like Oxford." But it has always, even when it was an agreeable place to live in, tended to play the part of Martha to Edinburgh's Mary — a part, indeed, that Edinburgh no longer plays very convincingly. "They were far behind in Glasgow," says a writer in the late eighteenth-century, "not only in their manner of living, but in those accomplishments and in that taste which belong to people of opulence, much more to persons of education. There were only a few families of ancient citizens who pretended to be gentlemen, and a few others, who were recent settlers there, who had obtained wealth and consideration in trade. The rest were shopkeepers and mechanics, or successful pedlars. It was usual for sons of merchants to attend the college for one or two years . . . (but) there was neither a teacher of French nor of music in town. The young ladies were entirely without accomplishments, and had nothing to recommend them but good looks and fine clothes, for their manners were ungainly." It is an unkind thing to say, but I fancy some points in this description still hit home. A lack of intellectual outlet, perhaps, helps to explain the conduct of that intelligent and interesting Glasgow murderess, Madeleine Smith. Glasgow, on the whole, still does rather despise the things of the mind. Its character and traditions are recent and composite, its social tone is set by good-natured people who have made money, and who want to live comfortably in the pleasant residential suburbs in the outskirts of the town, without being stirred up by ideas; by these, and by its vigorous, hard-drinking, combative, and humorous working classes. Glasgow should be the moral capital of Scotland, but, because it despises intellectuality, is not so. Yet it has character. It abounds in its own sort of life. And if it were ever to have the leisure to develop its own sort of culture, that culture would have nothing derivative, imitative, or provincial about it. The Glasgow comedians, indeed, already represent the elements of a folk-culture in the making.

Provinciality: that is a sore point with all Scotsmen. The word can have an aptness. Though Scotsmen, and particularly modern Scottish Nationalists, are reluctant to admit the fact, the most important foreign influence on Scottish manners and customs, throughout the centuries, has, of course, been that of England. Mrs Janet Roberts, in her delightful book, "Life Among The Scots", says of Queen Margaret, the wife of Malcolm Canmore: "She called her sons by English names, discouraged Gaelic, and frowned upon the Celtic Church. Stitching copes, chasubles, and altar-cloths with 'certain women of noble birth', she was perhaps the first to make the Scots feel provincial." During the Three Hundred Years' War with England, the Lowlands were occupied for years at a time by English armies. It is to contact with English soldiers, and with English favourites at the Scottish court, that the historian Hector Boece ascribes the decay of Gaelic — though in his time Gaelic was still the language of about half the people of Scotland: "Be frequent and daily cumpany of thaim (i.e. the English) we began to rute their langage and superflew maneris in oure breistis; throw quhilk the virtew and temperance of our eldaris began to be of litil estimatioun amang us." Yet Middle Scots developed into a very different sort of language from Middle English; and it was at the height of its development when Middle English had begun to decline. We can see the sinewy strength of the literary language of sixteenth century Scotland from this version of the Lord's Prayer: "O our Father quilk is in Hevinnis. Thy name mot be hallowit. Thy kingdom mot cum. Thy will mot be done in erd, as it is in hevin. Geve us this day our daylie breid. And forgyff us our dettis as we forgyfe our dettoris. And lede us nocht in tempatioun. Bot delyver us fra evil. Sa be it." The Scottish Reformers, however, were agents not only of English policy, but of English culture (Cardinal Bethune, whom they murdered at St Andrews, was the last strong leader of the old Nationalist Party which worked for independence of England and an alliance with France). John Knox wrote in the literary language not of contemporary Lowland Scotland, but of contemporary England, in spite of the protests of older men, who would grumble, "I knappe not your Suddroun" ("I have not got the hang of your Southern dialect"). There was never a Bible in literary Lowland Scots, and the Bible, for Scotsmen of the seventeenth century, was the most important of all books. Moreover, when the Court, and the more ambitious of the Scottish nobles, moved to England, Lowland Scots lost social prestige; it was revived by writers like Allan Ramsay, Fergusson, and Burns who could not claim to be gentlemen.

Salutation Hotel, Perth

One of the least provincial of Scotsmen, the philosopher and historian David Hume, was troubled by the paradox of the Scottish renaissance of the eighteenth century — a renaissance which, as Voltaire said, gave Europe laws about everything from landscape gardening to the epic poem — even though the epic poems are now unreadable, and though we cannot now very much admire "Capability" Brown's clumsy attempts, in landscape gardening, at the formal picturesque. "Is it not strange," Hume wrote, "that at a time when we have lost our Princes, our Parliaments, our independent Government, even the presence of our chief Nobility, are unhappy in our Accent and Pronunciation, speak a very corrupt dialect of the Tongue which we make use of; is it not strange, I say, in these Circumstances, we shou'd really be the People most distinguished for Literature in Europe?" Mrs Roberts, from whom I take some of these quotations, also cites the gloomy remark made in 1847 by the great Scottish lawyer, Lord Cockburn: "The eighteenth was the last Scottish century." It was to the eighteenth century that Scott and Stevenson tended to hark back, while John Buchan, at his best a worthy successor to Stevenson in the fast-moving historical romance, was perhaps most at home in the seventeenth century. Probably most modern Scotsmen, seeking nostalgically for an ideal period in Scottish history, find themselves thinking of the reign of James IV, the time of the Makars. But late mediaeval historians, like Hector Boece, were already lamenting the decay of the Scottish tradition, and the earliest scrap of extant verse in Lowland Scots, "When Alisaundre our King was deid", is itself a lament for the good old days. Scotsmen are, and always have been, great harkers back. There is some encouragement to be got, by a Scotsman who looks at things realistically, from this perpetual chorus of lamentation. For, after all, the Scottish character does very vigorously survive. All these English influences, when they cross the Border, are somehow transformed. Scottish culture remains something very easily recognisable, if not easily definable.

Scottish culture is now in the throes of a vigorous and conscious revival. The language problem, not unnaturally, obsesses the younger Scottish writers. There are attempts, of which I thoroughly approve, to "mak' the Lallans Hielan'", to extend the appeal of Gaelic and the Celtic tradition generally. There are attempts, of whose outcome I feel less certain, to remould Lowland Scots into a contemporary literary language, not so much by developing any existing rural dialect, as by combining the vocabularies of them all, and by enriching them with borrowings from the Makars and words from German, French, Gaelic and other contemporary languages; a great deal of translation of classical European texts into

Lowland Scots is being done, especially by that leading Scottish Nationalist, Mr Douglas Young. The difficulty about "synthetic Scots", as Mr McDiarmid once called it — the more fashionable term to-day is "Lallans" — is that the finest texts surviving are in Middle Scots, an archaic language, reflecting the ideas of a society which, however much one may regret it, is gone for good, and that the most vigorous living dialects, such as Buchan, reflect the narrow range of interests of an uncultivated peasantry. There is in fact a vocabulary in Lallans to express the rarified sentiments of Courtly Love, or the mediaeval obsession with Sin and Death, and there is a living spoken vocabulary — that of the Aberdeenshire "Bothy Ballads" — admirable for the purposes of realistic pastoral; but there is no vocabulary to express the interests of modern town life, or the complicated predicaments of the modern intellectual. The late Lewis Grassic Gibbon attempted a compromise by writing a trilogy of novels, dealing with town and country life in the North-East Lowlands, in English with a great many Scottish words woven in, and with a rhythm and syntax which imitated the peculiarities of Scottish speech: but it is doubtful whether even he achieved anything more than realistic pastoral; his characters, even when he takes them into the towns, remain simple, and perhaps over-simplified, country folk. Mr Fred Urquhart, who has written brilliantly about the lives of poor people in Scottish towns, does not use Scots except in dialogue, and this is also true of Mrs Willa Muir's two interesting novels about Scottish small-town life. Mr Hugh McDiarmid, the chief champion of a revived Lowland Scots, does not use Lallans much in prose, and his longer and more didactic poems tend to be chiefly in English.

I have no hostile feelings about Lowland Scots, but my own feeling is that there is also a special Scottish use of English, that has its own value. Nor, perhaps, should we Scots be too self-conscious about our special system of phonetics, the pure vowels which we substitute for Southern English diphthongs, and our "r's" which are pronounced at the ends of words, when there is an "r", and are not pronounced when there is not an "r" there (so that we do not say either "bettah" or "Victoriar"), and which are rolled rather than fricative. A very great poet like Yeats is full of rhymes and emphases that suggest the Dublin brogue, and the burr of such a rhyme as this,

> What voice more sweet than hers
>
> When young and beautiful
>
> She rode to harriers?

though it is pleasing to a Scottish ear is, I imagine, lost on most Englishmen. The English language, in fact, cannot any longer be considered as Southern England's private property; nobody objects when a famous American poet like Robert Frost rhymes — like an Elizabethan, though not like a modern Englishman — "been" with "in", and to appreciate the good work that is being done in verse and prose in the English language, not only by Americans, but by Scotsmen, Irishmen, and Welshmen, one must have a catholic attitude both to idiom and phonetics. (The Scots idiom in the use of English is as distinctive as the Scots system of phonetics. It is more formal and concise than the Southern English idiom. A Scotsman asks you to direct him to the station, an Englishman wonders if you can tell him how to get to it). It is the very flexibility of the English language, its aptness to take the impress of many national temperaments, that makes it such a universal medium. We speak of the American language, meaning the distinctive twist which the American environment, the American racial mixture, the American temperament has given to the English spoken in the United States, and in this sense the English spoken in Scotland should count, with Gaelic and Lallans, as a third Scottish language. It is by developing along its own lines, rather than by imitating current English models, that this language is likely to progress.

Scottish culture underwent a sort of eclipse in the nineteenth century after the death of Sir Walter Scott. Scott, like so many of his countrymen, was a harker back; he deserves the gratitude of all Scotsmen for interpreting the various Scottish regions, the Highlands as well as the Borders, the towns as well as the countryside, and the various Scottish traditions, the Whig as well as the Jacobite tradition, the Puritan as well as the Cavalier, not only to Europe, but to each other. But he did not look forward, he was most at home, as in "Waverley", in the period "sixty years since". He had no vision of the industrial revolution, of the depopulation of the Highlands, which, even in his own time, were beginning to transform his country, and his romantic picture of Scotland, which lodged itself firmly in the Scottish mind, became, as time passed, less and less related to current facts. Robert Louis Stevenson who could write, as in "The Wrecker", excellent contemporary sketches of Paris and San Francisco, never managed to perform exactly that service for his own Edinburgh; like Scott, he was obsessed by Scotland's past, and, since it was now a more remote past, he produced something that was more of a fancy picture. On the other hand, Scottish writers of the last two hundred years, like Burns or George Douglas Brown, who have had a more realistic vision than Scott and Stevenson, have tended also to have a narrower and more

St. Cuthberts Burial Ground,
Edinburgh

regional scope. The only inclusive picture of Scotland that is available for the enquiring visitor is, really, the romantic one. It is also the only inclusive picture for most Scotsmen themselves, if they have not the time and leisure, by a detailed study of history, to construct their own.

Yet the present position of Scottish culture — or, more broadly, of Scottish self-awareness — is a hopeful one. There are half a dozen or so young and promising poets — in Gaelic, in Lowland Scots, and in English, and there are several periodicals, two of them at least very handsomely produced, devoted to Scottish art and letters. Two young and prominent painters, Robert MacBryde and Robert Colquhoun, though working in London, are very much in the main Scots tradition — a favourite theme of theirs being the harsh and touching faces of old Scots beggar-women. There is at least one publisher in Scotland who devotes most of his paper to the younger Scottish writer. In Glasgow, the Glasgow Citizens' Theatre puts on and makes a financial success of new plays, by Scotsmen, on Scottish themes. The Saltire Society in Edinburgh is doing much to propagate a wider popular knowledge and understanding of Scotland's past.

There has always been in Scotland — the ballads are an example, so, in spite of its comic side, is such an institution as Burns Night — a very much more widespread *popular* feeling for culture than in England. W. S. Graham once described to me how, on a Saturday night in Lanarkshire, a drunken miner got on to the top of a bus beside him, and began to sing, in a husky but sweet and true voice, Burns's beautiful song, "The Lea Rig": the equivalent would be a tipsy English labourer singing "Greensleeves" in the London tube. Again, as Mrs Roberts points out, one finds douce Glasgow business men who have gathered, purely for their own pleasure, and using their own natural judgement, excellent collections of French pictures; and Miss Cranston, whose tea-rooms are a famous institution in Glasgow, entrusted her interior decoration to that radical experimentalist, the architect of the Glasgow Art School, C. R. Mackintosh. There are, of course, very many Scotsmen, as there are very many Englishmen, who have no conscious interest in culture at all. But culture, where it is present in a Scotsman, can never be a mere social veneer. The Scotsman is as passionate, as energetic, and as thorough, when he takes up poetry, art, or music, as he traditionally is about religion, soldiering, drinking, ship-building, and football.

The Scottish art whose tradition is most in need of radical and intelligent revival is probably architecture. The most impressive buildings in Scotland are the ruined mediaeval monasteries — ruined more by English vandalism than by reforming zeal — and the great square grim castles of the same period, like Borthwick. Towards the end of the seventeenth century, Scottish noblemen, no longer considering their castles primarily as places of defence, began to ornament and develop them in a very elaborate way. The most famous example of this early romantic style is Glamis. Defoe described it admiringly, as it stood at the beginning of the eighteenth century: "It is one of the finest palaces in Scotland. When you see it at a distance, it looks not like a town, but like a city . . . . The whole exterior is profusely adorned with sculpture, pinnacles, pepper-box turrets" — he means ogees — and Patrick, first Earl of Strathmore, who started to improve Glamis about 1670, observes complacently: "It is hardly possible by any description I can now make to give any impression to posterity of what this place was like when I first began my reformations." A smaller, chaster, and perhaps pleasanter example of the same style is Craigievar Castle in Aberdeenshire. The nineteenth-century Scottish Baronial style, of which Balmoral Castle is a famous example, derived largely from this seventeenth-century style, and from the novels of Sir Walter Scott; the rather false and fussy romanticism of the Scottish Baronial style casts its shadow back on buildings like Glamis, making their elaborations seem rather false and fussy, too. In towns like Glasgow and Edinburgh, from the latter part of the eighteenth century onward, a classicising, and latterly a hellenising tendency prevailed; modern Scottish critics of architecture, like Mr. John Tonge, seem to feel that though the classical parts of Edinburgh and Glasgow are admirable in their way they are not distinctively Scottish. In Edinburgh, it is certainly the high-piled rookeries of the Old Town, rather than the classical buildings of the New Town, that have a distinctively Scottish flavour.

Mr Tonge picks out (as a special example of what Scottish architecture ought to be) a late mediaeval building, heavily ornamented, Rosslyn Collegiate Church, near Edinburgh. "The ornament," he writes, "is Celtic — not archaistic, but adapting intertwining coils and the rest to mediaeval ends. The makers of Rosslyn did with English Gothic what the Makars did with the English tongue. Precisely the same juxtaposition of incongruous motives, the same crowded but firmly controlled ornament, is found in William Dunbar's aureate diction. And like Dunbar — Rosslyn is either warmly admired, or as heartily hated." On the other hand, Sir John Stirling Maxwell, a more cautious and pedestrian, but certainly a very scholarly critic, *does* manage to give a lukewarm verdict on Rosslyn: he thinks the ornamentation bold and ingenious, in its general effect, but rather coarse and clumsy, when it is looked into in detail. And there is nothing else at all like Rosslyn in Scotland, it has the air of being a "sport".

Map by Christopher Saxton, 1607
(after G. Mercator, 1595)
Loaned by P. J. Radford, Fareham

What all visitors to Scotland will find very pleasing is the old idiom of domestic architecture, which can be very well seen, for example, in the small coastal villages of Fife; the crow-stepped gables, occasionally turned towards the street, the sash windows, the steeply inclined roofs, the outside stairs leading to the first storey, the pleasant harl or rubble surfaces. The Scottish tradition in architecture is certainly not one of abstract symmetry, of what a modern Scottish poet calls "*bourgeois* geometries", and in that sense the classicism of the late eighteenth and nineteenth century in the towns meant a break with tradition. On the other hand, it is not a tradition of excessive ornamentation either — Glamis, to most judgments, is less impressive than earlier, simpler castles like Borthwick or Caerlaverock, Rosslyn than Glasgow Cathedral or St Magnus Cathedral in the Orkneys. The tradition is rather one of rugged and uncompromising fitness for a purpose, within a given setting; in that sense, a building like Mackintosh's Glasgow Art School is well within the tradition. The late Sir Robert Lorimer who designed the Scottish National War Memorial in Edinburgh, was a conscious reviver of this tradition, in his beautiful Thistle Chapel in St Giles' Cathedral, and in various large country houses. What Scotland specially needs at the moment, however — when all the bigger towns are in the throes of slum clearance and are eating up their hinterlands with new housing schemes — is a distinctively native idiom in the more modest types of domestic architecture.

One way to learn to understand and love a country is to leave it. Scotland, I think, really began to crystallise for me in Africa. The high plateau of Eritrea, eight thousand feet up, with its shabby, pleasant little provincial capital of Asmara, is approached by winding mountain roads, offering panoramas which dwarf anything offered by the worn granitic stumps of the Scottish Highlands; but these reddish mountains, peppered with small green trees, these goatherds leaning on their spears, these dried-up water courses, glimpsed far below in Gorges which the Diesel train passes over, offered no very exact points of comparison with Scotland; any more than the endless scrub of the Sudan, seen for days from the train in the tedious journey by the Nile Valley route from Cairo to Asmara, really could recall, except by mere featurelessness, the great brown boggy stretches of moorland in Sutherlandshire. The similarities that really struck home were at once more remote and more precise. Thus, in Eritrea, one hot Sunday afternoon, when I walked through the little village of Decamere, and found the shops all shut, no one about, only some hens scrabbling in the street, a goat chewing newspapers, an Italian woman, in decent Sunday black, taking out her child for a ride in his go-cart . . . . pushing the go-cart a little in front of her, so that it ran for a yard or two by itself, while the child in pleasure clapped its hands . . . . and two long-legged Italian schoolboys, kicking stones along the pavement, who paused for a moment to get a good look at the stranger, I might, for a moment, on a long Sunday walk, have been passing through some Scottish country village. There, too, I would have met that pervading stillness, these few walkers, these inquisitive eyes. And when I walked beyond that Scottish village, and looked back at its little lights, as it began to get dark, I would have felt a sense, as I did watching Decamere from a rubbish dump where the scavenger hawks whirled above me, of cosy sadness. I would have been aware of decent and limited lives, of the narrow routine which, because it makes every slight change in the routine a real excitement, keeps the soul alive. It is the very homely things about Scotland, I think, that touch the exile most. "The auld hoose, the auld hoose, what tho' the rooms were wee?"

Then again, on the one leave which I took during my early service in the Middle East, which was in Jerusalem, I felt almost back in Scotland. In Jerusalem, the old City, within its famous walls, is the East; and with its stalls of spices and its winding narrow streets, it is, in spite of the Wailing Wall and the Holy Sepulchre, the Arabic East. But the neat, new housing schemes of modern Jerusalem, so grey and so sedate, had an air about them of similar drab and decent housing schemes in new working-class districts in Aberdeen; and the Jewish boys and girls who, with nowhere to go, walked up and down one of the main streets on a Saturday evening recalled young people walking up and down, with a similar strenuous lack of purpose, on Union Street in Aberdeen on a Sunday; for, after all, the Scottish Sunday is modelled on the Jewish Sabbath. I understood why a Scottish friend of mine, trained in the old strict Presbyterian tradition — and if he had exchanged that for anything else, it was only for the equally strict and stern tradition of Marxian Socialism — told me that he had never felt more at home, during his ten years in the Middle East, in which he had wandered from Syria to Ethiopia, that when staying with Jewish friends in Palestine. The colours of Palestine, the light greens, the olive greys, the scratched limestone whites of the winding hilly roads, are certainly not very Scottish; but there is a sparseness and sharpness, a spare elegance in the contours of the country, that appeals very deeply to a Scotsman. And Scotsmen tend to feel an immediate moral sympathy with the laborious earnestness of the Jewish pioneers.

After all, the Old Testament, for the Scots, as for the Jews, is an especially sacred book. It appeals to the Scots largely because, in the history of the ancient Hebrews, clinging to their harsh but lovely homeland, threatened always by more powerful enemies, poor, proud, laborious, believing themselves a people who bear the burden of a special divine command, a chosen people, the Scots see an emblem of their own history. For the Scots, as for the Jews, the divine purpose is to be understood as it expresses itself in history, and history is to be understood as it expresses the divine purpose; the sense of history, for both peoples, is a religious sense. The history of mediaeval Scotland, the long struggle for freedom, the triumph at Bannockburn, the disaster at Flodden, the acceptance by a people of burdens greater than they can bear, is, in particular, a religious history. After Bannockburn a whole people rejoices, after Flodden a whole people mourns. The history of Wallace reminds us of the story of Samson; the history of Bruce reminds us of the story of David. As for the Covenanters of the seventeenth century, with their barbarous battle cry of "Jesus and no quarter!" they must certainly be set against the background of the Old Testament, the book whose stories and whose phrases were never out of their minds. Calvin, with his notion of election, had revived, for an imaginative people like the Scots, the notion of a chosen people. The religion of the Covenanters was no longer, as was even the gloomiest religion of the Middle Ages, humanistic. For them, men were like trees, and the whole forest, in Samuel Rutherford's phrase, had been sold to death. The architecture, the science, the literature of the "century of genius" had no more appeal to them than the marvels of Babylon to the Jews of the captivity. The Catholics, the Episcopalians, the English Independents were simply Philistines to be smitten with the sword, and, if any survived, to be made into hewers of wood and drawers of water. This religion left no middle ground between presumption and despair. Either a man had an inner conviction of election, or he was eternally rejected, and the eternally rejected might as well be destroyed. Nor did the military folly, the political absurdity of such ambitions matter, because the Lord was on the side of his chosen, and, at some crisis of battle, the Inspiration of a Minister of the Gospel was more worth attending to than the calculations of a General. Thus these miserable and exalted men rushed on their own destruction. They *were* exalted. Rutherford, rejecting any notion of universal salvation, has sublimity of a kind: "Every man hath conversion and new birth," he says, "But it is not leel come (loyally come by); they had never a sick night for sin; conversion came to them in a night dream: In a word, hell will be empty at the day of Judgement, and heaven panged full."

The seventeenth century, certainly, was Scotland's sick night for sin; but the dream was of a few saved and many, many damned. It was in the

Barbara Jones

Canongate Church.
Edinburgh.

end for Scotland a more disastrous and desperate dream — being a presumptuous dream, which bred despair in too many — than the dream of universal salvation, of hell eternally existent, but eternally empty, against which Rutherford directs his tremendous ironies. There is nothing that we can admire to-day in this smoky fervour that burns up the heart. Yet it was something in the Scottish temperament that fed itself on Calvinism, rather than something which Calvinism called into existence. The greatness of a nation may sometimes be based on qualities that we cannot much like or admire in the individual members of that nation; and it is doubtful whether, without this streak of presumptuous pride and barbarous fierceness in them, the Scots would have retained their independence throughout the long, agonising, three hundred years' struggle against England in the Middle Ages. This smoky fervour has been a quality of many great and unlovely Scotsmen from John Knox to that ambiguous thunderer, Thomas Carlyle; it is a quality that is something like the rage and unction of the Hebrew prophets. Much of Scottish history must, at any rate, be read by this mirky light. We should remember, too, that as well as this tendency to be eaten up by the zeal of God's house, the Scots have also some of the more amiable and admirable qualities of the ancient Hebrews: courage, laboriousness, strong family loyalties and affections, an unquestioning respect for their elders. Yet they have this grimness, too.

Yet there is another and very different side to the Scottish temperament, an almost physical delight in natural beauty, springing largely from the abrupt and vivid changes of the Scottish climate. Hamish Henderson writes to me from Arisaig how the pleasant mildness of a winter day there — a time when, in London, we are all huddling from the cold — could take away the sting from eternal damnation; and in Arisaig, as in the Highlands generally, eternal damnation, like arbitrary election, is still a living idea, which moulds men's lives. It did not need Calvin, indeed, to make damnation a living idea for Scotsmen of a religious temperament. "All erdly joy returns in pain", says Dunbar; but the seventeenth century, with its grimness, repressed the expression of that "erdly joy" which Dunbar and the other Makars, refreshed by a Scottish springtime, could convey so well. There is a note in Dunbar's poetry, when he greets the spring, that in later Scottish history will be almost wholly lost:

> The morrow was mild and meek, the mavis did sing,
> And all removit was the mist, and the mead smellit;
> Silver shouris doun shook, as the sheen crystal,
> And birds shouted in shaw, with their schill notis,
> The golden glitterand gleamis so gladit their heartis . . .

There is sheer physical exaltation here, in the new damp smell of the fields, the shrillness of the birds, the fresh shining look of everything, spring's noisy gladness. Such passages, and it would be possible to cite many more, suggest that there is a capacity for joy in the Scotsman that has never been fully developed.

Scotland, in fact, as Andrew Lang says, had the Reformation without the High Renaissance. Yet the Reformation is not wholly to be blamed for the nipping and chilling of such shoots of joy in the Scottish soul, for it did correspond to something already deeply rooted in that soul. Even in the brilliant court of James IV, as Mrs Roberts points out, "we already see certain characteristics that are usually credited to Calvinism. There is the Scottish Sunday, and James refusing to ride for any consideration, not even to Mass. There is the concentration on results, the suspicion of pleasure for pleasure's sake; James ordained that whereas shooting and archery be practised, and wapinschaws held four times a year, there should be 'no football, golf, or other such unprofitable sports.' There is the Scottish censoriousness: James, reports the Spanish Ambassador, has given up his love-making, not only 'from fear of God, but also from fear of scandal in this world, which is thought very much of here.' " The Scotsman runs to fierce extremes. He recognises himself in the Covenanters, with their harsh repression of the flesh, and in Burns, with his unbridled yielding to it. He does not think of striking a mean; and it does not occur to him that extremes are always less consistent than they look, that if the Covenanters suppressed the passion of lust, they had not suppressed the passions of pride and vindictiveness, and that if Burns was able to let his appetites run wild without doing himself mortal hurt, it was because he had rather strictly civilized his emotions. The humanist notion of the balanced and harmonious personality has, in fact, never had sufficient sway in Scotland, and certainly any possible Scottish humanism would be a very different thing from the easy-going, intuitive humanism of England. Scotsmen tend to admire a one-sided energy. And Scottish energy, even though it has something almost savage about it, has on occasion been tremendously creative; it does, however, tend to spring from a fundamental unbalance. The personal problem of many young intelligent Scotsmen to-day is conditioned by this situation — by the need, in a disordered world, of aiming at a certain inner balance and harmony, without cutting utterly adrift from a tradition which tends to destroy these. Scottish energy has been too often a blind energy; the young men want to give it eyes. But the principles of a specifically Scottish humanism have yet to be worked out.

One way, as I have said, to learn to love and understand a country is to leave it. Distance shapes elements which seemed discrepant or unrelated at the time of their immediacy into a new and illuminating perspective. In Africa, late at night, when I had been working alone, I would try sometimes to refresh myself, before resuming my task, by shaping in my mind the Scottish town which I know and love best, Aberdeen: I would recall the peculiar glitter of mica, on the granite frontages, on a frosty day; or, on a spring night, the blue bulb of a lamp at Holborn Junction, the branch projected under its shine covered not with buds but with blue bubbles; I would let memory trail a lazy finger along the run of the beach between the Dee and Don, touching the big white dance hall, the ugly red brick baths, the slums and the gasworks behind the shore, and behind the slums the glittering granite length of Union Street, the sunken gardens at Union Bridge, the pigeons fluttering above them, and then the grey terraces of Albyn Place, the substantial granite villas of Queen's road, at the tram terminus the big park of Hazlehead, its woods and golf-course running away into moorland, and beyond that again, a country road and quiet fields and farms. I was reassured by the sense of the continued physical existence of all that. It is the sense of the physical existence of a country that a book of this sort should convey; and in writing it I have attempted, as it were, to run over Scotland in imagination and touch its solidities with my hands. But it is to the real Scotland, whose aspect he will find in the photographs in this volume, that I wish to direct the reader's attention — not to the imaginary map of it in my head. The map is only useful in so far as it is a projection of the reality. Like all imaginary projections, such a map will distort much and omit much; it will have fulfilled its purpose, and can be flung aside, when it has given the reader some notions of the shape and dimensions — not only in space but in time, and not only in space and time, but in the world of spiritual values — of a real place. No single mind can grasp or express the whole reality of Scotland; but it is only the reality, in so far as we *can* grasp it, that can interest us at all.

Chapter 1

THE BORDER AND GALLOWAY

It is in the Border region and in Galloway that a modern traveller can get the firmest grip on what, in its great days, the Scottish Kingdom was. In the Highlands, he finds more striking, if not perhaps essentially more beautiful scenery, but he finds also the remnants of a patriarchal society in the last stages of decay. In Glasgow, and across the whole broad industrial belt, he finds a mixed population, Highland and Lowland strains running into each other, and a strong undigested dose of Irishry, and he discovers that local traditions and characteristics have been pretty thoroughly ironed out; Ayrshire, for instance, provides many cheery and rowdy holiday resorts, like Troon, for Glasgow folk; but there is little enough in the people's life and speech to remind one that this is the Burns country. In the north-eastern coastal region from Fife to Moray, the traveller would find a more definite local character, but a bleak landscape, an unforthcoming folk. In Edinburgh, against a magnificent stage setting, he would discover a people weighed down by the burden of their respectability and aping, in their speech, an idea of English refinement. In the Border region, and in Galloway, however, the traveller will find a settled agricultural and pastoral society, with local industries, like the weaving of tweed, based on local resources; and in yearly ceremonies like The Braw Lad's Gathering or the Common Ridings, he will find the sense of the Scottish past still alive.

Here, too, the shells of the great abbeys, like Melrose, and the more solid ruins of the strong and sombre castles. like Hermitage, can remind us of how noble and tragic that past was. The triple profile of the Eildon Hills recalls the tale of True Thomas, and the kiss he got from the Queen of Fair Elfland under the Eildon Tree, and all the magic in these Border ballads, their faraway quality, that springs — not really paradoxically — from a great closeness to the earth. Moreover, above the whole green landscape, there broods the spirit of that crippled genius, that "gigantic dwarf", as Balzac called him, Sir Walter Scott. Abbotsford must be seen, that "incoherent design," as Sir John Stirling Maxwell calls it, in which "Sir Walter.... despite his brilliant historical gifts, tolerated an ignorant medley of styles which he would have been the first to detect and to deride in any other medium." (Would he? He wrote about Scotland, and particularly about Scotland in the eighteenth century, with close and loving knowledge. But when he writes about other places and other periods, does he not often commit the same sort of blunder that one marks at Abbotsford?) Indeed, there is a danger of seeing the whole Border region through a haze of literature, with some tag from the ballads for ever ringing in one's ears:

> She sought him east, she sought him west,
> She sought him braid and narrow;
> Syne, in the clifting of a craig,
> She found him drowned in Yarrow.

Yet, in fact, the Border region has a purely visual beauty that need not depend at all for its effects on such associations.

The Ballads, in fact, unless we have read them with some knowledge of history, with some idea of the sort of society that produced them, may give us a misleading notion of what to look for in the Border region. The life of the people here is earthy and hearty; and the number of great houses and the popularity of the expensive sport of fox-hunting make it a less democratic life, a more traditional and pastoral one, than is to be discovered elsewhere in Scotland, except in the Highlands. It is not in the Border region that we should look for signs of the well-known radicalism of the Scot. Defending fox-hunting, and the social patterns that go with it, a Border journalist, Mr Robin Jay, after making it clear that he does not excessively love a lord, goes on: "I do care enormously for the easy relationship that hunting encourages between peer and plough-man, landlord and tenant, brewer and beer-drinker. I rejoice that because of hunting the Border landscape is plotted and pieced by great stout hedges and grey stone walls instead of the infernal, hideous, and strictly utlitarian wire fence of more progressive provinces. And I am also delighted to think that so long as there are still foxhounds the old mansions that look so benignantly through ancient woods at the trippers and the charabancs will still have a wisp of smoke around the chimney head, and jobs for grooms, and strappers, and gamekeepers, and gardeners." Speaking also of the Merse, the fertile agricultural plain of Roxburgh and Berwick — the rest of the Border counties are more given over to rough upland pasture for sheep — Mr Jay dwells appreciatively on the deep generous soil, the bumper crops of barley and potatoes. The solid, rustic, settled life he describes may seem to be at a far cry from the magic of the ballads.

Yet that, too, is an earthy magic, the magic of a peasant people, who see strange things in the gloaming. It is in a familiar country dialect, and with a naive peasant cunning that reveals its wiles, (for she is too proud of them to conceal them even from her victim), that the Queen of Fair Elfland speaks to True Thomas:

"Harp and carp, Thomas," she said,
"Harp and carp along wi' me;
And if ye dare to kiss my lips
Sure of your bodie I will be."

It is with a peasant's fatalism, yielding to the fulness of the blood and the impulse of the twilight, that he answers her:

"Betide me weal, betide me woe,
That wird sall never daunten me."
Syne he has kissed her rosy lips
All underneath the Eildon tree.

And in the most tremendous verses of that ballad, all the things named are common and elemental things: rivers, night, sun, moon, the sea, starlight, blood: which is what gives the verses their power:

O they rade on, and farther on,
And they waded rivers abune the knee,
And they saw neither sun nor moon,
But they heard the roaring of the sea.

It was mirk, mirk night, there was nae starlight,
They waded thro' red blude to the knee;
For a' the blude that's shed on earth
Rins through the springs o' that countrie.

Set the magic against the background of the real. The Border men, of the period when that ballad was composed, must often enough, on moonless nights, after some murderous raid, have forded rivers on horseback, the water splashing up to their knees. In the silence and the dark, the one thing to trouble their minds may have been the distant lapping of the sea. And with murder on their souls, they must often have felt, in the uncanny and dangerous dark, that they were wading through blood. We know the strong effect of these verses on us. What can their effect have been on these cruel, brave, violent men, to whom every image had such an awful intimacy? One thing is certain about these men; however crude and wrong the pattern of their lives was, it was informed with a sense of style, which conveys itself immediately in the ballads. Is there the same sense of style in the lives of Mr Jay's farmers, ploughmen, gamekeepers, shepherds, and hunting peers? We do not know, but at least on the Border the social and economic complications have not been introduced that make such a sense of style impossible — that make style possible only as a deliberate, cultivated, individual thing. Certainly, alas, the ballad is dead; but perhaps not the ballad atmosphere; and certainly not the ballad landscape.

The beauty of that landscape is not a coarse or obvious one. Washington Irving, a typical specimen of the literary traveller, seeing nature through the spectacles of books, was disappointed with the Border. "With mute surprise . . . . almost with disappointment," he found himself staring at a "succession of grey waving hills, line beyond line, as far as my eye could reach, monotonous in their aspect, and so destitute of trees that one could almost see a stout fly walking along their profile; and far-famed Tweed appeared a naked stream, flowing between bare hills, without a tree or thicket on its banks." There are trees and thickets now; stout hedgerows in the valleys, sparser conifers on the uplands. But to a more perceptive eye, that bareness would have been a beauty. The Southern Uplands are delicately modulated; their fluent and precise curves are really far more pleasing to the eye than, for instance, the lofty but monotonous ridges of the Cairngorms. The Border landscape gives one a sense of exquisite peace; its colours, its greys and greens, and purples, are as modulated as its shape. The sheep graze on the coarse pasture of the uplands, the quiet farms lie sleepily in the dales, the small towns nestle in the curve of a river, under the shadow of a hill: the very names of the little rivers, the tributaries of the Tweed and Teviot, are a sleepy music — Gala Water, Annan Water, Liddel, Yarrow, Jed. Yet, if we think of history, this is a deceptive beauty, like the beauty of the Border ballads themselves, which makes us forget that their themes, when they are not those of pastoral magic, are those of violence, of cruelty, of unrelenting feud. (This note, of course, does not belong uniquely to the Border. Aberdeenshire had the same turbulent nobility, and for a certain sinister gaiety the Aberdeenshire ballads are perhaps unsurpassed even by anything the Border can offer:

> Inverey cam' doun Deeside, whistlin' and playin';
> He was at brave Brackley's yates ere it was dawin'.
>
> Says, 'Baron of Brackley, are ye within?
> There's sharp swords at your yate will gar your blood spin . . . .')

Border ballads, and these ballads of Aberdeenshire, unlike English ballads, rarely compromise with passion for the sake of a happy ending. That is why, unlike English ballads, they produce all the effects of great poetry.

The Border, in fact, was till the Union of the Crowns the most disturbed region in Scotland. The great abbeys, with their promise of culture and peace, were mostly founded at a period before the Three Hundred Years' War with England, which secured the independence of Scotland, but secured it at a considerable price. The more solid castles, like Hermitage, often date, in their present form, from the fifteenth century, when the truce with England was comparatively secure. The smaller and cruder peel towers reflect the average uncertainty and brutishness of life on the Border during the greater part of the Middle Ages. It was a period of raids, to and fro, across the English border; and of forays and blood feuds among the Scottish Borderers themselves. The bellicose mood of these days is well expressed in the ballad of "Kinmont Willie", a Border hero rescued by the Scots, in an extraordinarily daring expedition, from the English in Carlisle: a ballad full of chaff and good humour — but where the Warden cries that, were there war between the lands (but, he adds piously, if unconvincingly, there is peace, and may peace remain!) —

I would ding Carlisle Castle doon.....
And slocken it sae wi' Inglis blude
That never a man in Cumberland
Would ken whaur Carlisle Castle stude.

James V hanged a few of these Border rievers, including the famous Johnny Armstrong. But it was not till James VI of Scotland and I of England created a militia, prepared to keep the peace by rough and ready methods, that law and order came finally to the region.

The Border towns were in a particularly difficult position. They were right in the track of any English invasion (the once flourishing town and strong castle of Roxburgh have vanished, because the Scots found that this position was untenable). The immediate neighbours of these towns, the arrogant Border nobles, Hopes, Kerrs, Musgraves, Armstrongs, Elliots, were neither particularly friendly nor particularly trustworthy. The Stewart Kings of Scotland found it advantageous to give these towns grants of land, which it would be their duty and interest to defend against any aggression. It was thus that there grew up the custom of the yearly Common Riding, in early summer, to mark the limits of the town's common lands, which is still celebrated at Hawick, Selkirk, Peebles, Langholm and Lauder. (At Galashiels, there is a rather similar ceremony called The Braw Lad's Gathering). The Provosts and Magistrates ride round the town moors and town farms to make sure that no powerful neighbour has been shifting the boundary stones; and the ceremony is an occasion for a town holiday, with horse-racing on the moors, bonfires, and dancing in the streets, as well as community-singing of traditional airs, specially associated with the town's history. Nowhere else in Scotland is it possible to see the *perfervidum ingenium Scotorum* turned, in this fashion, to the purposes of public and official merry-making. The Common Ridings are as near as can be to Scottish carnival.

The aspect of the past, as well as its ceremonies, is very much alive on the Border. The four great Abbeys, Melrose, Dryburgh, Kelso, and Jedburgh, have suffered, more through war and neglect than through fanaticism; but they are magnificent even in their ruins. Kelso Abbey, founded in 1128, is, like the almost contemporary and better preserved Abbey of Dunfermline, a fine example of Norman work, with rounded arches in most places, though a pointed arch in the great central tower marks the transition to early Gothic. Its design is peculiar in that the choir, now demolished, had several bays, while the nave and transepts had only one each, while above the crossing-place of these four arms there is a very high tower, open to the church; the interior must thus have given an impression of enormous height, contrasting with rather restricted floor space. Jedburgh, which became an abbey in 1147 after some years as a priory, contrasts strongly in its general plan with Kelso: it has a rather long nave, and a rather short choir. The pointed arch is more frequent in Jedburgh, and in what remains of Dryburgh all the arches are pointed; Dryburgh is beautifully sited, on a wooded slope, above a bend of the Tweed, and is an appropriate resting place for Sir Walter Scott, who so much loved that river. Of all the four great abbeys, Melrose had the most chequered history. It was completely destroyed by Edward II when, with unfortunate results for himself, he invaded Scotland in 1332, and, after being partly restored by Robert the Bruce, was again partly destroyed by Richard II in 1385. Melrose once more grew to greatness and beauty during the 15th Century, but it was finally destroyed by yet another English army, under Hertford, in 1545. Scottish historians are apt to dwell with some complacency on these facts, and to give the Scottish Reformers credit for leaving Melrose alone; but no doubt the Scottish Reformers would have worked their will on Melrose, if the English had left them anything worth destroying. Even in its ruins, Melrose, particularly in the delicate tracery of its windows, remains the best example in Scotland of the decorated style of the later Middle Ages.

Of castles in the Border region and in Galloway, two of the most imposing are Hermitage, on the middle border, and the triangular castle of Caerlaverock, by the Solway shore. Hermitage, with its great square wings, its massive walls of dressed stone, is a very striking building, and Sir John

Stirling Maxwell considers this, and the rather similar Borthwick, farther north, to be, in their grim way, the two most imposing buildings in Scotland. Caerlaverock's triangular plan (a gatehouse flanked with drum towers at the apex, and a drum tower at each of the other two corners) is interesting and unusual. Galloway, like the Border region, has its fair share of antiquities. Sweetheart Abbey, which the wife of John Balliol, Devorgilla, built to house the heart of her husband, is more picturesquely situated than any of the Border Abbeys. Rising out of trim green lawns, its walls of rosy sandstone look across the Solway Firth to the Cumberland hills; it is, seen from a certain distance, probably the most delightful ruin in Scotland; but when it is considered in detail, its design and workmanship appear coarse, compared to those of Melrose. Lincluden Abbey in Kircudbright, on the other hand, one of the earliest collegiate churches in Scotland, has tracery equal to that of Melrose. Galloway, however, attracts visitors not so much for its ruins as for its quiet pleasant towns — Kircudbright, which is a haunt of painters, and Newton Stewart, coiled in a bend of the Cree — and for its fine and quite unexpected mountain scenery. The coastline of the Solway Firth is, like that of most broad firths, rather smooth and uneventful, the coastal plain is rich with fat farms, but beyond Newton Stewart lies the region of the Galloway hills, of which the highest, Merrick, looks over the Firth of Clyde, the peaks of Arran, and the rocky speck of Ailsa Craig: it is even possible to make out the hazy outline of the Irish Coast. Merrick towers to the south over a series of lochs, terraced each below the other, Enoch, Neldricken, Valley, Trool; while behind it to the north-east stretches a glaciated valley at the end of which lies the five-mile-long Loch Doon. This whole area of hill and loch is like some displaced fragment of the Highlands; and it draws a great deal of its charm from the contrast with the rich, fat, sleepy, typically Lowland plain, from which it rises quite abruptly. Galloway has been throughout Scottish history a rather isolated region, and it is rather isolated even now. Ayrshire farther north, and already much affected by industrialisation, is full of favourite holiday haunts for Glasgow people, but Galloway is almost unknown to them; it attracts, however, discerning visitors from England. There is a Welsh strain in the people here, and the region bred some of the most fervent Covenanters: Caerlaverock Castle fell to them, after a long siege, in 1641.

To know these regions of Southern Scotland well is not to know all Scotland. For the problems of modern Scotland are chiefly the problems of the industrial revolution, and here, as in the north-east, the full impact of that movement has been evaded. Nor does the pattern of agrarian life in this region, attractive as it is, really offer any solution to the problems of the industrial belt: what Glasgow, like other great industrial cities, has need of is not a tradition which has been quite definitely destroyed, but an order which has never been achieved. The problems of industrial Scotland cannot be solved, any more than industrial problems anywhere else, in terms merely of national history. Yet Scotland's national history has been noble and tragic; even if it has now been resolved into a wider pattern, it ought not to be utterly forgotten; and this region of Southern Scotland is its best memorial.

A lonely white-washed farm, sheltered by a tree, against the bare,
rolling curves of the Merrick, near Loch Trool, Kircudbrightshire. *British Council*

This pack-horse bridge on Gala Water,
has the old-world note that typifies Border scenery. *British Council*

above: St. Abb's Head, Berwickshire —
one of many rocky East Coast fishing havens
that brave the bleak North Sea. *British Council*

The smooth curving lines of the beach at Drummore,
Wigtownshire, are typical of the Solway coast.
British Council

right: With its L-shaped construction, The Academy, Borgue,
Kircudbrightshire, recalls the traditional layout of a
Scottish castle. *Will F. Taylor*

Thirlestone Castle, Berwickshire: note ogee towers,
corbellings, ornamental battlements, all typical of the
Scottish seventeenth century. *The Times*

A street in Lochmaben, Dumfriesshire.
The wide avenue of low simple houses
converges gracefully on the neat Tolbooth tower. *British Council*

Characteristic of the Border landscape,
with its low, bare, elegant lines, is Birkhill Pass, Dumfriesshire. *Will F. Taylor*

The quiet of the Borders: a hamlet of low houses nestling cosily in a nook of the
Lammermuir Hills. *Will F. Taylor*

Jedburgh Abbey: the west door of nave, splendidly massive, with round arch, and repeated recessions. *Will F. Taylor*

Sweetheart Abbey, in Dumfriesshire, founded by Devorgilla of Galloway in memory of her husband,
has one of the finest sites of any of the Border abbeys. *Will F. Taylor*

...olbooth tower. *E. W. Tattersall*

...t, Kircudbrightshire. *Will F. Taylor*

...*dam*

47

The Border landscape at ts suavest and most romantic, at St Mary's Loch, near Tibbie Sheils. *Will F. Taylor*

Typical of the gales of the Scottish East Coast is this wild spray of water at North Berwick. *Balmain*

Clustered pillars and pointed Gothic arches, in a corner of Melrose Abbey, one of the most famous of Border ruins. *E. O. Hoppé*

Melrose Abbey, from the north west, with the cloister garth in the foreground. *Will F. Taylor*

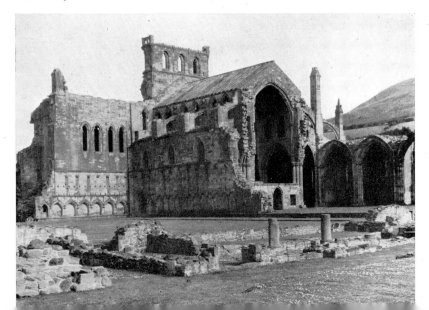

49

left: The old Border Bridge (built in 1642) at Berwick on Tweed. Berwick, which changed hands thirteen times before 1482, is now an English town, but its county, Berwickshire, is Scottish. *Mustograph Agency*

Thomas Carlyle's birthplace at Ecclefechan, Dumfriesshire, with its sash windows, and passage into a courtyard, is typical of Border domestic architecture. *Will F. Taylor*

right: Delicate and strong clustered pillars at Dundrennan Abbey, in Kircudbrightshire. *Will F. Taylor*

St. Andrew's Tower, Peebles, restored in 1882, is the only remains of a church built in 1195 and twice destroyed by English armies. *Reece Winstone*

This quaint figure of James I of Scotland, in the grounds of Dryburgh Abbey, was erected, with a companion figure of James II on the other side of the obelisk, by the Earl of Buchan in 1794. *Reece Winstone*

The triple crest of the Eildon Hills from Bemersyde, the ancestral
home of the Haigs. This was Sir Walter Scott's favourite view. *Alfred Furness*

Another of the charming old Border bridges: over the Nith, at Dumfries. *Robert M. Adam*

Chapter 2

EDINBURGH AND ITS NEIGHBOURHOOD

"F_{ew} places, if any," says Stevenson, "offer a more barbaric display of contrasts to the eye. In the very midst, stands one of the most satisfactory crags in nature — a Bass Rock upon dry land, rooted in a garden, shaken by passing trains, carrying a crown of battlements and turrets, and describing its warlike shadow over the liveliest and brightest thoroughfare of the new town. From their smoky bee-hives, ten stories high, the unwashed look down upon the open squares and gardens of the wealthy; and gay people sunning themselves along Princes Street . . . . see, across a gardened valley set with statues, where the washings of the old town flutter in the breeze at its high windows."

It is in such highly picturesque terms that the first impact of Princes Street is usually described. Yet the north side of the road, on which people generally walk, looking across at the gorge of Princes Street Gardens and the Castle above them, is, in the words of Mr George Scott Moncrieff, a "gimcrack jumble of horrid shops"; Miss Cicely Hamilton has said that the effect of Princes Street is rather as if one side of Kensington High Street had been torn away, to reveal an incredibly romantic panorama. The statues in Princes Street Gardens, of which Stevenson speaks, are not very good statues; the most conspicuous memorial there, that to Scott, was described by Dickens as "the spire of a Gothic church taken off and stuck into the ground." The Nor' Loch, in which the castle once romantically reflected itself, has been drained and turned into a railway cutting; though most visitors seem to feel that the rumbling of the trains, as they go by, somehow adds to the total romantic effect. But can that be said of the North British Hotel, at the east end of Princes Street, which is one of the first buildings that strikes the eye of the visitor getting out of the train? In the words of Mr James Bone, whose "The Perambulator in Edinburgh" is one of the pleasantest books about the city, "Too prosperous for a white elephant, not handsome enough for a giraffe" — it has a huge high tower — "it puts the Calton Hill completely out of scale and ruins Edinburgh's most delicate piece of architecture — the Register House of Robert Adam. Nearly all that was gained by the good sense of old Playfair, who kept the National Gallery and the Royal Academy at a low elevation, so that they lie like graceful classical ornaments on the bosom of the city, is undone by this abnormal growth." Add to all this that the Castle itself is a mixed, haphazard collection of buildings, with no particular unity of style. Does the peculiar magic of Princes Street remain?

It does, for it is essentially, as Stevenson saw, a barbaric effect. It is the great rock, seen across the gorge of Princes Street Gardens, that makes it, that and the profiles of the "high-piled rookeries" of the Old Town. That the Castle itself is a jumble is all to the good; it appears almost a natural stony outcrop, growing from the volcanic rock. Nor does the mixed and often mediocre architecture of the north side of Princes Street really matter; even if it were all in the best Georgian manner, like some of the crescents of Bath, or the squares of Dublin, it would be merely a touch of classical detail in a total picture that is utterly romantic. Princes Street is like a stage setting for some tremendous drama, and when, at one o'clock in the afternoon, a time gun is fired in the Half-Moon Battery on the Castle Rock, it is like the thrilling words of Fortinbras, that bring down the curtain on "Hamlet": "Go, bid the soldiers shoot!" The total effect of Princes Street might be compared to that of a paragraph by Thomas Carlyle; every detail may seem garish and exaggerated, but the ensemble is exciting. The nipping and eager air, the rumbling of trains, the rattling of trams, all help to sustain this exhilaration. And even Miss Hamilton, when she compared Princes Street to High Street, Kensington, admitted that the people of Edinburgh walk with a briskness, an air of dash and purpose, and eye each other with a frank curiosity, which is not common among the natives of South-West London. The street, for the Scotsman, is a place of encounter. "People walking in Princes Street at night," says James Bone, "especially on early winter nights when a slight mist from the valley exaggerates the craggy heights of the Old Town and gives its lights a richer glow, its darkness a murky grandeur, may sometimes have wondered, as they lifted their eyes towards them, what was behind those little golden spots that stamp so strange an arabesque on the Edinburgh night. The warmly clad promenaders, however, have other business on hand: the challenge of eyes . . ."

Much of the history of Scotland can be understood by contrasting the old Town, lying on the ridge between Edinburgh Castle and Holyrood Palace on the lower slopes of Arthur's Seat, with the New Town, of fine squares and solid public buildings, the town of the Adams and Playfair, that lies behind the north side of Princes Street. It was through the Old Town,

Moray Place, Edinburgh.
Eighteenth Century

that Matthew Bramble entered Edinburgh: "We had only an imperfect view of the Castle and upper parts of the town, which varied incessantly according to the inflexions of the road, and exhibited the appearance of detached spires and turrets, belonging to some magnificent edifice in ruins .... The city stands upon two hills, and the bottom between them; and with all its defects may very well pass for the capital of a moderate kingdom .. .."

Crusty old Matt goes on to describe life in the huddled tenements, or "lands", of the Old Town: buildings which as early as the seventeenth century, because of the narrowness of the ridge on which the Old Town is built, had shot up, like skyscrapers in Manhattan for similar reasons, astonishingly high. "What first strikes the nose shall be nameless," says Bramble's nephew, Melford, "but what first strikes the eye is the unconscionable height of the houses, which generally rise five, six, seven, and eight stories, and in some places (as I am assured) to twelve." The steep slope from which these tenements rise makes their height more imposing still. They cannot, at any time, have been pleasant to live in. "Every story," says Matthew Bramble, "is a complete house, occupied by a separate family; and the stair, being common to them all, is generally left in a filthy condition; a man must tread with great circumspection to get safe housed with unpolluted shoes . . . You are no stranger to their method of discharging all their impurities from their windows, at a certain hour of the night, as the custom is in Spain, Portugal, and some parts of France and Italy." Passers by would be warned of the descent of this ordure by the cry, "Gardy loo!" and the streets were swept by scavengers before morning. Still, life in the Old Town must have demanded a strong stomach. In Smollett's own time, the rich were already striving to get away from these picturesque but smelly quarters. In Stevenson's time, they had long since become, what they remain to this day, a slum, of which the shell is attractive to antiquarians. "Here," he says, "in the narrowest of the entry, you find a great old mansion still erect, with some insignia of its former state — some scutcheon, some holy or courageous motto, on the lintel. The local antiquary points out where famous and well-born people had their lodging; and, as you look, out pops the head of a slatternly woman from the Countess's window."

Yet it is the Old Town which still dominates Edinburgh. It speaks for an older Scotland, its sharp, twisty streets, its broken irregular profiles, its towering heights, all suggest the noble and tragic Scotland of the Middle Ages; as do, indeed, the names in this district — Lawnmarket, Grassmarket, Cowgate. It grew up, packed, cramped, towering, in the days when the great King across the border was a patient, a deadly, and an unremitting enemy; the houses still seem to be huddled round the Castle protection; the profile that one sees from Princes Street is dramatic and expectant. The New Town, with what Mr Robert Garioch calls its "bourgeois geometries", the town of the Adams and of Playfair, the "modern Athens", reflects a quite different Scotland, that of the Whiggamores, of those who had made their peace with England, and it is no accident that one of Edinburgh's finest classical buildings, Robert Adam's Register House, with its graceful corner cupolas and its urbane facade, was paid for out of moneys forfeited from Jacobite estates after the '45.

What the Castle is for the Old Town, Calton Hill tries to be for the New. It is crowned with a number of monuments, which show an eager if rather undiscriminating classicising enthusiasm; there is a national monument, unfinished — it has been dubbed "the Modern Ruin" — to the Scottish dead of the Napoleonic Wars, modelled on a peristyle of the Parthenon; modelled on the Athenian monument to Lysicrates, there is a monument to Dugald Stewart, one of the many illustrious obscure of Scotland's past, a late eighteenth-century moral and mental philosopher; and there is a tower commemorating Lord Nelson, modelled, according to Stevenson either on a butter-tub or a spy-glass. Is this all a little comic? Perhaps. Yet there was nothing essentially comic in Edinburgh's intellectual revival in the eighteenth-century, Whiggish though its main impulse was; if that Edinburgh was taken in by "Ossian", if it clapped its hands at a dull tragedy by a Scottish clergyman, crying, "Whaur's yer Wullie Shakespeare, noo?", still it appreciated David Hume at his true worth, it extended a welcome to Burns, and Burns's predecessors, Allan Ramsay, Fergusson, had already found shelter there. In Edinburgh, too, flourished these Presbyterian moderates who (in the teeth of illiterate and malevolent fanatics, like Burns's Holy Willie) were striving to give Calvinism a humane and ethical tinge, to connect religion with the duties, and even with the graces of common life. In architecture, though not in the atmosphere of ordinary intellectual life, this classical impulse lasted well into the nine-teenth century. The patronage, kindly if ill-informed, of the Prince Regent, and the novels of Sir Walter Scott, led Lowlanders to dress themselves up as Highlanders, and to dwell sentimentally on the manners and customs of those whom their ancestors had feared as dangerous barbarians; Carlyle, and Stirling who purported to reveal "The Secret of Hegel", denounced Hume, and the whole rational tradition of the eighteenth-century as doggedly as any Holy Willie; Presbyterianism itself soon lost all rational-ising impulses; respectability came to imply obscurantism; but though elsewhere in Scotland, the turbid romanticism of the Victorian age expressed itself in a suitable architectural idiom, Scottish Baronial, in Edinburgh the classical tradition in architecture stood firm throughout the nineteenth century. Playfair, the last great inheritor of the tradition finished his building for the Royal Scottish Academy in 1823, for the Scottish National Gallery in 1859. Nobody can deny the handsomeness of these bridges, streets, and squares, these solid bank frontages, in the New Town, that reflect the spirit of the classical revival. Yet Edinburgh, unlike Dublin, does not leave on the mind the impression of being a predominantly Georgian city. The Old Town still towers over the New, dwarfs and dominates it, where in Dublin, for instance, the elegant self-assurance of Merrion Square or College Green is quite unruffled by the existence of the two great Cathedrals. In the classical idiom (and not merely in that idiom as applied to architecture) eighteenth-century Ireland found the expression of a national mood; Curran and Grattan could suffuse a prose which now seems to us stilted and artificial with anger and with pathos, they could use, as Burke could, the very stiffness and ornateness of a rhetorical manner to heighten the effect of their eloquence; and when we look at the facades of the fine Georgian streets in Dublin, the "grey eighteenth-century houses" of which Yeats spoke, we can never forget that they have been, time and again, a fitting and noble background to national tragedy. Whig Edinburgh was prudent enough to avert tragedy; even the best Scottish prose of the eighteenth-century, the prose of Hume, is capable of expressing only an intellectual passion, a cold, obstinate self-sufficiency, a scorn for fools; and there is something of this deadly coldness about classical Edinburgh. The idiom that in Dublin expresses the discovery of a national mood, in Edinburgh expresses the surrender of one. The most scholarly of recent Scottish architects, Sir Robert Lorimer, in the National War Memorial on Castle Rock — in which he did not, however, have a free hand — in the big private houses which he built, and in what is perhaps his masterpiece, the Thistle Chapel in St Giles' Cathedral, went back to older models. "No one regrets." says Mr George Scott Moncrieff, "the classical era that gave us the fine buildings of Bruce, the Adams, Playfair, but it should not act as an insuperable barrier to our taking up again the unexhausted tradition of earlier times, the essential simplicity of which lends itself admirably to the needs of the day."

Something should be said about the people of Edinburgh. They have a reputation, in other parts of Scotland, for painstaking gentility, and Mr George Malcolm Thomson has some cruel observations on their attempts to speak elegant English. Aware, he says, that "cawstle" is wrong, but that "castle" is better than "cestle", they occasionally, in their transitional periods, flounder into strange locutions, such as "gaws-mesk." It is true that the middle classes, and especially the professional middle classes, seem to set the note in Edinburgh, where plain working folk set the note in Glasgow; one cannot imagine an Edinburgh Will Fyffe singing, "When I get a couple of drinks on a Saturday, Auld Reekie belangs tae me!" On the other hand, it is not true, as Glasgow people sometimes tend to think, that Edinburgh is a parasite city, consisting solely of lawyers, doctors, teachers, ministers, and decayed literary men; Edinburgh is the chief centre of the fine printing industry in the United Kingdom and one of the

Charles I and Old Parliament House
Edinburgh

main centres of the brewing trade; and one of the most elegant crescents of the New Town, because it was chiefly favoured by Leith merchants, got the name of "Whisky Row." (Not that they drank a great deal of whisky, but that they made a great deal of money from it.) Yet it is true that the genteel tradition dominates. Scottish poets, in particular, have inveighed against it; from Fergusson, jeering at the respectability of the small shopkeeper, strutting out in his "guid braid cloth", to Mr Hugh McDiarmid, in a tone of rage and love,

> till I saw all these people
> As specialists in hates and frustrations, students of helpless rages . . . .
> All emotionally suspended and dubious . . . .
> (Their powers of speech all hopelessly misapplied)
> Because their talk evaded, deserted, their real theme . . . .
> All who could help to open the way for true expression —
> The teachers, the ministers, the writers — are living like maggots
> On dead words in an advanced state of decomposition
> — For most of the important words were killed in the First World War —

And Edinburgh has not given birth to new words yet
In which it can say anything worth saying, make anything but animal
(noises.

Edinburgh — but Edinburgh is no worse than anywhere else . . . .
Is this tradition, indeed, so deadly? I know only three Edinburgh people
well. One, a working-class boy, had struggled and schooled himself to
speak this stiff, false English; in the Middle East, where I knew him, I
suppose at least it stood him in better stead than a dialect would have.
Another, though he is still apt to talk about "the inclement weather",
has adapted himself very gaily to the rough-and-tumble of the cinema
industry. The third, with the help, indeed, of St Andrews and Oxford,
has become quite the most affable and cultivated of my friends; he is
what the genteel tradition should be but isn't. There is, at least, in Edinburgh, this stiffness and falseness, an unfortunate thing. Character, certainly,
lies under it.

Edinburgh, from her volcanic ridge, has splendid views, looking northward
across the Firth of Forth to the Lomonds, eastward to the sea, south-west
to the Pentland Hills: views usually obscured by haze. She lies among rich
farming country, the Lothians, with their big and handsome farm houses,
and their dry soil, favouring oats, wheat, potatoes. The smaller towns
in the neighbourhood have their attractions; Linlithgow with its ruined
Royal Palace, Haddington with its bullet-scarred fourteenth century
church, Stirling, much farther up the Forth, holding the key to Fife and
the Highlands, with its sombre and dominating castle, more interesting
architecturally than Edinburgh's, enclosing as it does a palace block, a
palace block in the manner of the early Renaissance; but Stirling, except
for its castle, and some interesting old buildings, like Argyll's Lodging,
one of the earliest town-houses of the nobility, is a rather drab town.
Many Scottish towns, especially those that lie within the industrial belt,
are drab. It is against a predominantly rather bleak urban background
that the showiness of Edinburgh stands out. Little Marjorie Fleming, with
her usual smug aptness, expressed this quality of Edinburgh in a memorable
couplet (expressed, too, the well-doing gentility of its rich folk):

In a Conspicuous Town she lives
And to the poor her money gives.

Upon all who visit her, however vague their detailed observations may
be, Edinburgh leaves this impression: a Conspicuous Town.

Moray House, in the
Canongate, Edinburgh.
One of many quaint old
buildings in the Old
Town. *A. F. Kersting*

A general view of Princes
Street, looking west.
The turreted erection is
the Scott Memorial.
Behind it lies the
Royal Scottish Academy;
high to the left,
overlooking the scene,
the Castle. *Pictorial Press*

left: With its projecting
gables, this Canongate
house has not changed
much since the great
Reformer, John Knox;
lived there.
Donald McLeish

Melville Close,
Edinburgh: note the
gables thrusting out
from the roofs,
the crow-steps on one
of them, and the outside
stairs leading to second
stories. *British Council*

right: This view of
Edinburgh Castle,
through a narrow
passage-way, shows
these abrupt changes
in street and roof levels
which are part of
Edinburgh's charm.
Robert M. Adam

64

St. Giles Cathedral, with its Crown steeple, contrasts with the classical style of the other buildings in the High Street, Edinburgh. *Balmain*

opposite : Bakehouse Close, Edinburgh. These Old Town buildings, once fashionable, are now slums, many of them scheduled for demolition. *Valentine, Dundee*

Evening over Edinburgh: a view of the city from the Calton Hill. *Robert M. Adam*

A carving above a
doorway in the Cowgate.
The figures
with the barrel suggest that
this building was
connected with
the Coopers' Guild.
The carving
is dated 1643.
Reece Winstone

The similar insignia, above
another Cowgate doorway,
of the Edinburgh
Corporation of Tailors.
This carving is dated 1644.
Reece Winstone

The Calton Hill,
Edinburgh.
The memorial for the
Scottish dead of the
Napoleonic wars,
modelled on the Parthenon,
can be faintly seen.
A. F. Kersting

A view of the
perpendicular cliffs
of Arthur's Seat from
the high, huddled buildings
of the Old Town.
Reece Winstone

66

67

George Heriot's Hospital, Edinburgh, the famous school founded by "Jingling Geordie" Heriot, the goldsmith who was a friend of James 1. Note Renaissance ornamentation. *British Council*

The entrance gateway to Stirling Castle. The entrance towers are fifteenth century work, the palace on the left early sixteenth century, with interesting early Renaissance decoration. *Leonard & Marjorie Gayton*

Melville Street, Edinburgh: the terraced houses are an example of the classical style of the new town. *Balmain*

Canon Ball House, Edinburgh: the rubble surface, caused by a mixture of stones of different shapes and sizes, is typical of old Scottish buildings. *British Council*

The north aisle of Rosslyn Collegiate
Church, near Edinburgh,
the most elaborate Scottish example
of the late mediaeval decorated style,
heavy and intricately ornate.
A. F. Kersting

Carved stone-work from Rosslyn
Church representing the
Seven Acts of Mercy. *A. F. Kersting*

The strangely twisted and
skewlooking "prentice pillar"
in Rosslyn Chapel. *A. F. Kersting*

A capital from Rosslyn Chapel:
on left at the top, is a man
whistling with his fingers.
A. F. Kersting

The Forth Bridge,
from South Queensferry.
One of the most beautiful
railway bridges in the world. *Balmain*

The Old Bridge, Stirling —
one of the many solid yet graceful
old stone bridges with which Scotland,
a land of many rivers, abounds.
British Council

72

Jail Wynd, Stirling: note the square clock tower, with balustrade, ogee turret, and weather-vane.
Ursula Hartleben

Mars Walk, Stirling: old houses through a fine wrought-iron gate.
Ursula Hartleben

Old houses, with winding "public stairs", in St. John Street, near Stirling Castle.
Reece Winstone

left: Argyll's lodging, the largest of Scottish town houses, was built in 1630, by the Earl of Stirling, a well known poet, who died insolvent.
It then passed to the Argyll family, whose crest is carved over the windows.
Leonard & Marjorie Gayton

A typical old Scots farmyard, from a window of the Achray Hotel, near Edinburgh.
Ursula Hartleben

right: Another ogee turret on the Guildhall tower facing the Market Cross in Stirling. Note the crow-step gables. The date is 1669, the style typical of the seventeenth century.
Reece Winstone

left: North Berwick, on the coast near Edinburgh, is a paradise for golfers. The photograph shows the Firth of Forth and Fidra Island.
Balmain

The Village of Dean, Water of Leith Valley near Edinburgh : picturesque, with its winding cobbled street and old houses.
Robert M. Adam

right: These white-washed, tiled houses, one set behind the other on rising ground, at Cramond, Midlothian, are typical of village architecture in the Lothians.
Will. F. Taylor

This fountain at Linlithgow Royal Palace, built for James V in 1535, is a good example of the clumsy yet rich Scottish early Renaissance style.
Leonard & Marjorie Gayton

The Lothians are rich
country.
The slopes of the
Lammermuir hills from
Fields at Danskine,
East Lothian.
British Council

The River Tyne at
Haddington in East
Lothian.
At Giffordgate,
which lies to the left
of the bridge here,
John Knox was born.
Balmain

A beautiful Norman
Doorway at Dalmeny
Church,
near Edinburgh.
H. J. Smith

82   The Lammermuir Hills at Mayshiel, East Lothian. *British Council*

Another view of the Lammermuir Hills from a ploughed field, near Haddington. *Balmain*

Chapter 3

GLASGOW

$\mathbf{G}$lasgow is usually approached by
those who write about it in such a depressed frame of mind, that it is
worth saying, before getting down to the more sordid side, that it has
some very fine buildings, and even some very fine modern buildings.
Alexander Thomson, who designed many of the nineteenth century churches
and terraces, had an European reputation as an architect in the style of
the Greek revival, and he had competent followers. Unfortunately, as
Sir John Stirling Maxwell remarks, work in this style in Glasgow "suffers
a great deal from the material in which it was carried out and from the
dirt which has dulled it down. Designs so severe demand pleasing materials,
especially when the buildings are on a small scale. Had Portland stone
been available or a rosy sandstone, their beauty of proportion would have
been more evident, whereas in a cold grey stone they look gloomy and
out of place." Yet Thomson's severe and chaste churches seem particularly
suited to the sober mood of Presbyterian worship. Glasgow also contains
one modern building — Charles Rennie Mackintosh's School of Art
— which is internationally famous as one of the first attempts (he designed
and completed it between 1894 and 1904) at architectural functionalism.
It has appeared to some critics that its bold simplicity not only reaches
forward to Le Corbusier, but harks back to the older traditions of Scottish
architecture. Like the old Scottish castles, and unlike the work of the
classical revivalists in Edinburgh and Glasgow, it makes no attempt at
merely mechanical symmetry.

In spite of the fact that in the last century they demolished their old
University buildings, because of the slums which surrounded them, the
people of Glasgow are not, in fact, such philistines as the people of Dundee,
who as recently as 1931 destroyed their Town House, which was generally
considered one of the finest of William Adam's buildings. There are in
Glasgow odd and pleasant survivals of an older, simpler city, like Provand's

opposite : The huge frowning curtain wall of ruined Tantallon Castle,
near North Berwick, on the East Lothian coast. *Balmain*

Lordship, one of the manses of the Cathedral prebendaries in pre-Reformation times, which dates from the fifteenth century, and which, with its crow-step gables, its deep-set narrow windows, and the pleasant rough stonework of its thick walls, is an admirable sample of the older Scottish domestic architecture: while Glasgow Cathedral itself, though its lovely walls are blackened with industrial smoke, is the most complete and most impressive of surviving Scottish mediaeval cathedrals. It is a massive building. "Ah!" says Andrew Fairservice in Scott's "Rob Roy", "it's a brave kirk — nane o' yere whigmaleeries and curliewurlies and opensteek hems about it — a' solid, weel-jointed mason-wark, that will stand as lang as the warld, keep hands and gunpowther aff it." It is specially noted for the crypt on which, probably to make the best use of the sloping site, the choir is raised up; with its many pillars and its tense vaulting, it has all the mystery and complication of Gothic architecture at its best. It is easy, of course, to sigh over this past; but to visit the great shipbuilding yards along the Clyde is to realise that the passion for beautiful and accurate construction, which inspired Glasgow Cathedral, is still alive in the people, even though it no longer expresses itself in religious architecture. Neither the modern buildings of Glasgow University, on Gilmorehill — though their site is dramatic and excellent — nor the Corporation Art Galleries, in Kelvingrove Park, are particularly distinguished as architecture; but the latter is worth visiting for its collection of paintings by artists of the Glasgow School.

In the eighteenth century, when its main wealth came from the tobacco trade, Glasgow was generally considered by visitors to be the most spacious and well laid out of Scottish cities — a very pleasant contrast to the huddle of the Old Town in Edinburgh. The industrial revolution affected a complete transformation, and Alexander Smith, who died in 1867, expresses the atmosphere of the transformation. He is worth quoting at fair length: like many Scottish poets, writing in English, his handling of language leaves much to be desired, but he had the Scottish poet's gift of keeping his eye on the object. He expresses the dreariness, and yet the titanic impressiveness, of his swollen and furious city:

> Draw thy fierce streams of blinding ore,
> Smite on a thousand anvils, roar
> Down to the harbour bars;
> Smoulder in smoky sunsets, flare
> On rainy nights, with street and square
> Lie empty to the stars.

From terrace proud to alley base
I know thee as my mother's face.

When sunset bathes thee in his gold,
In wreaths of bronze thy sides are rolled,
Thy smoke is dusky fire;
And from the glory round thee poured,
A sunbeam like an angel's sword
Shivers upon a spire.
Thus have I watched thee, Terror! Dream!
While the blue Night crept up the stream.

The wild Train plunges in the hills,
He shrieks across the midnight rills;
Streams through the shifting glare,
The roar and flap of foundry fires,
That shake with light the sleeping shires;
And on the moorlands bare,
He sees afar a crown of light
Hang o'er thee in the hollow night.

These are the images that Glasgow conveys to a poet: I left Glasgow myself when I was not yet a poet but merely something similar, a child: and some of the images the word "Glasgow" conveys to me are childish. I remember as well as anything a shop at Anniesland where my mother used to buy me large, hard, awkwardly shaped sweets — "chough jeans", they are called, which means tough young women — that have to be sucked slowly away, and cannot be bitten at, nor even moved with the tongue in the mouth, so large they are, without the danger of breaking a tooth; I have never come across these formidable confections anywhere else. I have what I fancy is a completely romantic picture of suburban districts like Bearsden and Milngavie, where the neat, sharp, separate little houses seemed to me, after the red brick block of flats in which we lived in Broomhill, pathetically small and sweet. And I have wonderful memories of holidays in Glasgow's pleasure islands; Brodick in Arran, where there was a general store of corrugated iron, with a magically composite smell — oranges, liquorice, coffee, leather: perhaps even (I may be romancing, but it may also be that a child's senses are romantically acute) the tinny and wooden smells of pails and spades for the beach; Rothesay, with its horse trams, where I was first taken into a church, and wept, I remember, because it was not a picture house; Millport, with its little wooded hill, full of bluebells, from the height of which I would look down upon the sea; the chug, and the oily, pleasantly sickening smell of the old paddle steamers taking one to these places; the jolly sing-song of the trippers' voices: the wonderful and proletarian things to eat, which a Clydeside holiday entailed — fish and chips, drenched in vinegar, and eaten out of an old newspaper, and delicious fried mealy puddings, crisp and breaking in the hand: the open air pierrot pavilions, and the strenuous comedian, singing at the top of his voice (to some expert in popular song, does this date my childhood?):

> Eat more suet, eat more fru-it,
> Eat more apple pies,
> Eat whatever you darn well please,
> But you *must* take exercise!

All that was jolly, and garish, and vulgar, and good, about living in Glasgow: but there was the other, sadder image, the image of the labyrinth; and to the labyrinth I must return.

My father's family lived over at the other side of the city, near Langside, where Queen Mary lost a battle fateful for the future of Scottish history, and we used to go to see them on the tram — they still had, in these days, trams with open tops, or with open fronts to closed tops, and to ride out there, as they rattled along in the clammy weather, was to have a thrilling sense of vertigo and danger — and we used to pass through long miles, as it seemed to me, of dark depressing streets, in which particularly I noticed the muslin and beaded curtains on the tall, narrow windows of the tenements curtains yellow or grey with the smoke of that city, and shutting out, for those who lived behind them, what little light there was; and my favourite nightmare, till I started reading stories about witches, and cultivating more properly childish terrors, used to be one of wandering through these streets in the evening, with a vague but agonising sense of familiarity, seeking some landmark, finding nothing but the repetition of monotony, finding nothing strange and nothing known, seeking, and not finding, my own home. Too vividly also I remember (to-night, in London, the same light will fill me with sadness) the faint yellow flare of the lamps, and fainter of these dreary windows, through the smoke-tainted dark . . . .

Much later, I was to wander through these streets with a vivid and waking adolescent eye, noting the peculiarly human aesthetics of the slum. It is worth anyone's while to undertake such explorations; and the peculiar sense of loneliness and depression that will come over the explorer has its own moral value. He should note the bright and gaily arranged little

The Library, Glasgow Art School
Mackintosh, 1907

shop-windows, with their cheap sweets, tempting the eye rather than the palate, their cheap literature, their cheap, bright tasty things of all sorts; as if Christmas were always near, and always needed to be, so grim is the rest of the year; the social centres, the fish-and-chip shop, the ice-cream parlour, the public house: the women, with shawl and basket, standing talking to each other in the street; the men, lingering near the public library or the public lavatory, perhaps with a green football special in their hands, smoking some stump of cigarette — an "aifter", as a cigarette half-smoked, stubbed out, and lit again, is called in Scotland. This is a country of danger and frustration: I have been once, so long ago that I forget when or how, in one of these little tenement apartments, up so many stairs: an Irish family, steel engravings of bespectactled Popes, coloured prints of the Sacred Heart; old furniture, reflecting the elaborate bad taste of our grandfathers, decayed plush chairs; a pervading odour that was half kitchen and half sick-room; and a feeling that one should lower one's voice, as in a room where someone is dying — perhaps through the stained curtains there was so little light — though I think that nobody was dying, just there and then. And I remember, too, in my adolescent explorations of Glasgow, something that Edwin Muir has spoken of, the feeling of walking in a world of intense and brooding sexual passion. Under a railway arch, against sinister shadow, but flaring out itself, there would be a little shop window full of Boccaccio, Rabelais, Balzac's "Droll Stories", Margaret of Navarre, Paul de Kock — "your scrofulous French novel, in grey paper, on blunt type." There are, of course, such shops in every great city. But in Glasgow one notices these, and the obscene chemists, more vividly, because one has a sense, wandering in the labyrinth, of the huge grey frustration which, fallaciously, they promise to assuage.

Yet that cannot be anyone's final verdict on Glasgow. The explorer feels frustrated but it is not certain that all the natives do. It is the great melting-pot of the Scottish race; Highlander and Lowlander have merged here, and there are also modern immigrations, like that of the Irish, who, besides providing material for religious squabbles, for petty gang wars, and for unpleasantness at football matches, constitute in Scotland a social and economic problem rather like that of Italian immigrants in France — like the Italians, with a lower standard of living than their neighbours, they are willing to work harder for smaller wages, and often at duller or more unpleasant jobs; and, like Italian labourers in France, quite naturally they do not want to merge their own cultural identity in that of their neighbours. There have been other smaller immigrations, like that of the Lithuanians. There will, I suppose, be in Glasgow as elsewhere in Scotland in future a Polish element. There are Jews. In many ways, perhaps, the social pattern of working-class Glasgow is rather like that of the Bronx. (I was forgetting the Italians, themselves, who, not so numerous, tend to control here and elsewhere in Scotland the ice-cream saloons, which, in Scottish working-class districts as in the United States at large, are important social institutions for the young). A play like Elmer Rice's "Street Scene", which shows Americans of different national origins rubbing along as well as they can — not terribly well — in an unsalubrious quarter of Manhattan, would, I think, go down well with a Glasgow working-class audience.

What do all these people feel? They have not produced an art, a literature, a philosophy — any young man with talent gets out and away from the slums as soon as he can: and when he gets away he forgets, they have not yet produced anybody with the talent to write and the courage to remember. Yet, they have in a way expressed themselves. The great terrible city imposes on them a certain unity of style. They are affable and talkative, with an accent which, while nobody could say it has poetic beauty, lends itself very aptly to the work of the great Glasgow comedians. In such a comedian as Tommy Lorne Glasgow probably expressed a great deal of itself. Mr Colm Brogan, in a brilliant essay, has described his impact: "Tommy was tall and angular, and when he was dressed as a woman he was mostly bones and two mournful and apprehensive eyes. His Dame was a weel-daein' working-class woman, with a lot of jerky dignity, determined not to be put upon, but finding the world too much for her. She had beautiful squeals of indignation and moments of outraged stillness when she mutely asked Heaven if this or that outrage could be . . . ." (Tommy's actual words, when he folded his hands on his stomach, were — being Irish and devout, Mr Brogan does not give them — "In the name!")

There is this comic bewilderment: there is also pointless violence. I well remember being approached, one evening in Cairo, by a young Glasgow tough, already far gone in drink, who told me that he was one of the district leaders of the Billy Boys. Taking a fancy to me for some reason, he invited me to visit him at his headquarters in the Gorbals, where he would give me a royal welcome. He was an absurd young ruffian, but with an air of casual condescension which I did not find wholly unimpressive. Did I know, he asked me pugnaciously, who the Billy Boys were? Something, I said demurely, to do with King William and the Protestant Succession? His brow clouded; he was engaged, like some mediaeval bravo, in a feud so old and complex that he had forgotten its origins. Yes, yes he agreed, it was vaguely about that — slightly puzzled that an outsider should know or care: "But, man, it's mainly for sociability and self-protection!" And the main thing was that I should visit him, and if anybody in his district appeared to be on the point of bashing in my head, I had only to mention his name, which was, I gathered, talismanic. There was a real emotional magnanimity in his voice, a trembling sense of what was due to himself — he, a leader, must protect and succour the weak — and I did not find him wholly comic or hateful, though I knew that his manner of fighting was probably to get two friends to hold an enemy down and then to kick the enemy in the teeth. Perhaps among these silly Glasgow gangs the old feuds that clang and rattle through so much of Scottish history are being fought out at their last level. But I think it says something for the vigour of the Scottish stock that the slums of Glasgow should produce even toughs and comedians, and not merely creatures without hope. I would rather see, in any human being, a dangerous or a destructive sort of vitality, than a quiet no life at all; while there is life, there is hope, and I feel there is hope for Glasgow. Dr Walter Elliot has very aptly called Glasgow "the furious city"; in the great shipyards and foundries, that fury — which, indeed, has spread a thick black and smoky belt across the whole waist of Scotland! — has been constructive; I believe that we shall see a time when, in social life, too, its expression will be constructive energy. But at least Glasgow is not a dead city; fury, frustration, laughter, violence, these are the qualities of a living and savable soul.

Against the grey, huddled city, a graceful suspension bridge across the Clyde. *Margot Lubinski*

The heart of Glasgow, the City Chambers and the Cenotaph, floodlit and shining on a typically rainy night. *Margot Lubinski*

above: This panorama shows the magnitude of the second largest city in the British isles. Many landmarks can be recognised, Oakbank Hospital and St. Aloysius Chapel to the left, Trinity College and Park Church to the right. *A. D. S. Macpherson*

right: Though smoke-stained and huddled round by mean buildings, Glasgow Cathedral is one of the finest pieces of mediaeval architecture in Scotland.
George Outram & Co.

Belmont Terrace in Great Western Road. *A. F. Kersting*

97

A glimpse of the old Glasgow — a ground floor in Provand's Lordship, the house of one of the mediaeval Cathedral dignitaries. *A. F. Kersting*

A silhouette of Glasgow by night, showing the outlines. *H. Youngman*

opposite :   A photograph from the highest tower of the Trinity College. The small figures on Lynedoch Street below give some idea of its height. *A. D. S. Macpherson*

A dockland sunset on the Clyde. *Dorien Leigh*

The Clyde, before it is darkened and dramatised by Glasgow's grime, above Hyndford Bridge, Lanarkshire. *British Council*

opposite: Another view of Largs Bay, in winter sunshine. *A. K. Rittener*

On the West coast near Glasgow: looking across to the Cumbraes from above Largs Bay. *A. K. Rittener*

A walk along the esplanade, on a bleak but brilliant winter's day, at Largs Bay. *A. K. Rittener*

Industrialisation has not spoiled all Glasgow's neighbourhood. Lanarkshire suggests mining villages, but it has also rural oases like this field of daffodils at Carmichael House, Thankerton. *The Times*

Chapter 4

THE NORTH-EAST

"At Nairn," says Dr Johnson, "we may fix the verge of the Highlands; for here I first saw peat fires, and first heard the Erse language." From Nairn, down through Moray, Banff, Aberdeen, Kincardine, Angus, and the peninsular Kingdom of Fife, there is a low-lying region, facing the North Sea, which is like a north-eastern thrust of the main body of the Lowlands. With the stubborn Ochils at its rear, the Firth of Tay to the north, the Firth of Forth to the south, and guarded by Stirling, which is the strategic key to Scotland, being also the gateway to the Highlands, Fife has always been a particularly snug and protected region. Farther north, Aberdeenshire seems more exposed. But in the Town House at Aberdeen, you can see the armour of the Provost — a short, sturdy, bandy-legged man — who, in 1411, along with the Earl of Mar, defeated Donald of the Isles at the "Red Harlaw". That battle is generally taken as the last attempt of the Gaelic-speaking Highlanders to get a solid grip on the Lowlands. It can also, says Dr Agnes Muir Mackenzie, be understood as the first of the great clan feuds, between Mac-Donald and Stewart, with the Crown and England as interested parties. The Stewart Kings were never able to impose their notions of feudal order on the patriarchal society of the Highlanders. The two bases of society were, indeed, incompatible; on the one hand, a conditional loyalty, based on land tenure, on the other, an unconditional loyalty, based on kinship; and it was to the turbulence of the Highlands and the Islands that the English King was, throughout the Middle Ages, accustomed to appeal, when he sought for allies in Scotland against the Lowland monarchy. It is to the Lowlands, also, that the main credit of the successful Three Hundred Years' War, for independence, against English ambition, was due; and without this northward thrusting flank, guarding them against the Highlands, the Lowland Kings might have had a much more difficult task. These are the circumstances which gave this north-eastern region its historical importance, and which give it its present character. It is the least Celtic part of Scotland; the people of Aberdeenshire, in particular, are considered by other Scots, and not only by Highlanders, to have an almost

Prussian reserve. And to Scotsmen not in sympathy with the Highland tradition, Aberdeen often appears the ideal of a Scottish city. On the other hand, a Highland poet, Captain Hamish Henderson, once wrote to me in Egypt, "What are you writing? More tight-lipped poems for your Flemish town?" and when he visited Aberdeen lately, "A braw town, but too full of Whiggamores."

Aberdeenshire, or at least the coastal and agricultural region, Aberdeen and Buchan, is very bleak. For the full expression of that bleakness, it is better not to go to Aberdeen itself, but to such coastal fishing towns as Kinnaird or Peterhead. Peterhead, which is the most easterly point on the Scottish coast, sticks out into the cold North Sea like a raw red fist. It has a huge louring prison, and quarries of red granite, a painful rock, from which its houses are mostly built; even in the single day I spent there I found that colour hurtful to the eyes. Peterhead is so much exposed to the weather, that trees will hardly grow there, and those that I saw, cowering against a wall in the Manse garden, were twisted and stunted by the wind; a former Minister had built one garden wall full of holes, so that the wind would sough through it, and remind him, sometimes, of the pleasant rustling of branches. This bleak landscape has lately found a poet worthy of it, Mr George Bruce:

> This is the outermost edge of Buchan,
> Inland the sea birds range,
> The tree's leaf has salt upon it,
> The tree turns to the low stone wall.
> And here a promontory rises towards Norway,
> Irregular to the top of the thin grey grass
> Where the spindrift in storm lays its beads.
> The water plugs in the cliff sides,
> The gull cries from the clouds,
> This is the consummation of the plain.
>
> O impregnable and very ancient rock,
> Rejecting the violence of water,
> Ignoring its accumulations and strategy,
> You yield to history nothing.

I find that, thinking of the self-sufficiency as a region of Aberdeen and its bleak but fertile Buchan hinterland, I once said almost the same thing:

> This is the shape of a land that outlasts a strategy
> And is not to be taken with rhetoric or arms.

And a local proverb expresses, more concisely, part of the thought that was in both of our minds: "Aberdeen, an' twal mile roun, and then whaur are ye?"

Granite, a rock which is a mixture of quartz, felspar, and mica, is very hard and does not weather; time seems to make it barer and harder and brighter. The flakes of mica glitter, so that the granite of Aberdeen, on a bright frosty day, looks like spun sugar. Marischals College, the most ambitious modern building in Aberdeen, the masterpiece of the late Marshall Mackenzie, shows what can be done with this intractable material; you get at it through the narrow opening of Broad Street, passing the shabby buildings of "The Press and Journal", and once you are facing it, there is not enough space in front of it for you to get far enough back to see it properly. Aberdeen people are not really fond of Marischal College; they call it a piece of fretwork in granite. But I prefer the verdict of a scholar, the late Sir John Stirling Maxwell, who says, "Those who contrast with disapproval the severity of three stories of class-rooms and offices with the airy lacework of the parapets and pinnaces, do not grasp the nature of this imperishable rock, so unsuitable for the ornament that we are accustomed to see wrought in freestone, but capable of daring uses in which

The Albert Institute, Dundee. Nineteenth Century

the hardiest freestone would have but a short life...." The use of granite, indeed, gives a congruity and handsomeness to Aberdeen even where there is not this brilliance of construction; looking down Union Street, from the fine old Market Cross, you see no building which stands out strikingly from its neighbours, but there is a general effect of sober classical dignity which makes Union Street, after Princes Street, and in a completely opposite manner, the handsomest thoroughfare in Scotland. Many visitors, however, find Union Street too grand and glaring, and prefer the quieter, more traditional charm of Old Aberdeen. St Machar's Cathedral, there, which dates mainly from the fifteenth century, has a sturdy granite body, and two squat sandstone spires; its two square towers, with their corbelled parapets, suggest a castle as much as a church, and express the uncompromising strength of the Aberdonian character. King's College is interesting in that it has one of the only three crown steeples in Scotland (but it is less elaborate and beautiful than that of St Giles' Cathedral in Edinburgh, having only four arched supports where the latter has eight, and being topped with a cupola instead of a spire); Marshall Mackenzie's modern additions to King's College tone in exactly with the feeling of the older buildings, and, especially when contrasted with the daring originality of Marischal College, they show his versatility and taste. Aberdeen is perhaps more *itself* than any other city in Scotland; it has resisted the deadliest impact of the industrial revolution (its main industries are local and traditional ones, fishing, granite quarrying, and paper-making, which can make use of local water-power), just as it resisted Donald of the Isles, and Montrose when by force he imposed upon it, first the Covenant, and then a rejection of the Covenant. This strong self-containment does not please everybody. My friend Hamish Henderson calls it Whiggish. But if it is, I am afraid I admire it, and there is a strong dose of Whiggery in me.

The weather, the atmosphere, and the people's manner of speech soften as you go south. There are towns like Stonehaven, the county town of Kincardine, with its shingly beach, its neat little harbour, its houses and hotels piled high above the sea, where a writer feels that he could settle and write some novel, full of pastoral sentiment. Farther south, the Fifeshire fishing villages have, indeed, already attracted painters. It is out of half a dozen simple elements — steep roofs, crow-stepped gables, sometimes turned towards the street, well-proportioned sash windows, each sash divided into six panes, pleasant rough stonework, or whitewash, or harling, and outside stone stairs leading to a second storey — that the peculiar charm of Scottish village architecture is compounded. Add to that, in such fishing villages, the way the streets wind up and down above the little harbours, with their massive stone quays. There is nearly always something else of interest, too; like the tolbooth, or old jail, in Culross, whose square clock tower, thrusting up from the slope of the roof, is crowned with a graceful ogee; or like the sturdy little fifteenth century church, so admirable in its proportions, which faces the savage anger of the sea at St Monans.

The people of the Kingdom of Fife have, in contrast to those of Buchan, a soft, slurring speech, and a character that reveals itself not in such hard outline; they even appear a folk of devious nature, and the old proverb has it, "When ye sup wi' a Fifer, tak' a lang spoon." Some of the proverbs, indeed, in this region, have a rare pithiness. "He that will tae Cupar, maun tae Cupar", says one, and when I used to pass through that little grey town, with all its shops closed, with its glum boys standing at street corners, on a Sunday, on my way to St Andrews, I used to feel the force of that: only sheer thrawnness, I thought, could have driven the man in the proverb towards Cupar in the first place. But like many of these small Scottish towns, where one does not linger, Cupar may have its secret enchantment, if only one could stay to learn it. For the traveller in Scotland, it is still often as with Dr Johnson at Nairn: "We had no motive to stay longer than to breakfast, and went forward . . . ." But life, of a sort that one cannot stay to penetrate, lingers on in places from which one moves on with a sigh of relief.

About St Andrews itself, much has been written in a rather sentimental vein. It owes its charm not so much to its ruins, as to their associations: the remains of the cathedral, Mr George Scott Moncrieff describes as a "serration of stone tusks, before which the aching imagination sinks, incapable of visualising a great church"; St Rule's tower, on the other hand, one of five eleventh century square towers still standing in Scotland, is perfectly preserved; and St Salvator's College preserves, in great completeness, the Franciscan church of the same name built in 1456. Perhaps the best general impression of St Andrews is that conveyed, with his usual melancholy dignity, by Dr Johnson: "The cathedral, of which the foundations may be still traced, and a small part of the wall is standing, appears to have been a spacious and majestic building, not unsuitable to the primacy of the kingdom. Of the architecture, the poor remains can hardly exhibit, even to an artist, a sufficient specimen. It was demolished, as is well known, in the tumult and violence of Knox's reformation . . . . Not far from the cathedral, on the margin of the water, stands a fragment of the castle, in which the archbishop anciently resided. It was never very large, and was built with more attention to security than pleasure. Cardinal Beaton is said to have had workmen employed in improving its fortifications, at the time when he was murdered by the ruffians of the reformation, in the manner of which Knox has given what he himself calls a merry narrative . . . . The city of St Andrews, when it had lost its archiepiscopal preeminence, gradually decayed; one of its streets is now lost; and in those that remain, there is the silence and solitude of inactive indigence and gloomy depopulaton."

It would be unfair to describe modern St Andrews as inactive, indigent, gloomy, or depopulated; in term time, there are the students with their fresh, weather-chapped young Scotch faces, the wind teasing their red cloaks; in summer there are visitors, drawn mainly by the famous golf-courses; once a year, in spring, on Kate Kennedy's day, the students dress themselves up as famous figures out of the Scottish past, and go, on horseback, in coaches, and on foot, in proud procession round the town. Yet there is, in these streets sometimes, Johnson's silence and solitude; and there is an atmosphere about the place that recalls the gloomy cadences, heavy with the sense of mortality, of his prose. Andrew Lang caught that note,

> And still the thin and biting spray
> Drives down the melancholy street,
> And still endure, and still decay,
> Towers that the salt winds vainly beat.

And R. F. Murray,

> Oh, cruel off St Andrews Bay
> The winds are wont to blow!
> They either rest or gently play
> When there in dreams I go . . . .

The students themselves, I think, from my own memories of St Andrews, feel that atmosphere: they feel that this is a city of the young, and yet of the swiftly passing generations of the young, and of the young oppressed by an awareness of the past: "notre histoire est noble et tragique." That awareness was enhanced by the distinguished figures from the past whom, in my own time, one could see pottering about St Andrews, more rested and relaxed there than in other places, where history was too obviously moving on past them: Sir James Barrie or Mr Baldwin — as he still was; one would not have been really surprised to see Balfour, or Roseberry; and there were personages in the University itself (like the noble, lofty, and bearded apparition of Professor D'Arcy Thomson) that seemed to have outlasted time. Would the gossip, in these fine old houses in South Street, not be about Saintsbury, about Austin Dobson, about Stevenson, and about Andrew Lang? Death was not real, or was too real altogether. The elegance and the sadness of the place, weighted down with so much tradition, was something too subtle for the students, as raw as most Scotch students, always to catch the note of; but even protesting against that atmosphere, as sentimental, as unreal, one was affected by it, and talking, for instance, to students from Dundee (blustering uneasily that their ugly world was a real world) one had a sense of ironic superiority. Ironic, sad, frustrated, one still seemed to be in touch with a world of possible beauty:

> In dreams the year I linger through,
> In that familiar town,
> Where all the youth I ever knew
> Burned up and flickered down.

Ruins of St Andrews Cathedral

Nonsense, of course: what burned up and flickered down for me was not youth but the ardours, the frustrations, the sentimentalities of the awkward age . . . . but then that is an age that many Scotsmen never outgrow! Much, much of what one feels about St Andrews is sentimental accretion; yet I know, in my heart, that I remain accreted with that sentiment.

"Dundee is dust; and Aberdeen is a shell," says Hugh McDiarmid somewhere. Dundee is the third city in Scotland, a centre of the jute industry, noted for its resourceful female labour, famous for its jams, its marmalades, its cakes studded with almonds, its black indigestible Scotch bun; but it has no beauty that a man should desire it; it tore down its Town House, which was one of William Adam's best buildings, and it is mere chance, I suppose, that the fine steeple of its Town Church is still intact; it has no shape or soul, and some of its slums, as our photographs show, can compare with those of Glasgow. Even the famous Tay Bridge, which crosses the Firth of Tay, from Dundee to Fife, is disappointing; a lattice bridge, brick on iron piers, it is the longest of its kind in the world, 3,593 yards; but it does not begin to compare in impressiveness with the leaping girders of the much shorter Forth Bridge (just over a mile in length) farther south. It has been celebrated in verse by the hopelessly incoherent and clumsy Scottish poet, M'Gonigle, whose verse expresses, if anything does, the very soul of Dundee — a sad, floundering thing.

Yet if Dundee is even more shapeless than Glasgow, its people, like Glasgow people, are warm-hearted; I must not forget that in a Dundee man, during the war, I found one of my best and loyalest friends. Probably no place should be judged except from the inside. There is much in the North-East that I have passed over: the moors on Deeside and Donside which I have seen shimmering in the heat haze, the slim silver birches making a stipple with their small leaves against the sky: the quiet good taste of a town like Elgin, which Mr George Blake describes as "the best thing in the north-east": the fine Romanesque chapel and the quaint old houses at Leuchars; the special lives of the fisher-folk — Torry, in Aberdeen, is a district with its own appearance, its own dialect, its own way of life; or the sharp and shrewd wit of a people more sparing in their speech than any other people in Scotland. The impression that the life of the North-East makes, at its best, has been described in the case of a hinterland like Buchan as Scandinavian, in the case of a town like Aberdeen, and many of the small coastal towns farther south, as Flemish. But all that is merely to say that it does not correspond to a romantic idea of what Scottish behaviour should be. The North-East is very Scottish: bleak, hard, reliable: not easily responsive, but for those who have had patience to learn its ways, neither cold nor cruel.

With its pepper-pot
turrets, ornamental
battlements,
and corbellings,
Glamis Castle is the
most elaborate
example in Scotland
of romantic
seventeenth-century
castellation.
Donald McLeish

Contrasting with the
pretentiousness of
Glamis, the little
fourteenth-century
church of St. Monans,
set right against
the sea, has a
pleasing sturdiness.
*Leonard &
Marjorie Gayton*

A view of Auchmithie Harbour from the village. *Will F. Taylor*

right: The graceful Tolbooth at Culross in Fifeshire, *Leonard & Marjorie Gayton*

Though less known than the Border Abbeys. Dunfermline, (notice the great solid pillars and round arches) is better preserved than they. *Donald McLeish*

115

Pittenweem, another Fifeshire fishing village;
notice the outside stairs, leading to the second story. *Leonard & Marjorie Gayton*

right: A glimpse of Dundee's slumland:
a sidelight on hunger, order, and sanitation in the Scottish industrial area. *W. Suschitsky*

A street in Crail, Fifeshire, leading down to the harbour.
Notice tiled roofs, sash windows and crow-stepped gabling. *Leonard & Marjorie Gayton*

Agriculture, as well as fishing, thrives in Fifeshire: a view from a hill at Newburgh looking down on the Firth of Tay. *Will F. Taylor*

left: Contrasting sadly with the quaint old-world charm of small east coast towns like Culross, is this grim tenement scene from Dundee. *W. Suschitsky*

The Market Cross, the Tolbooth in the distance, and on the right a well-preserved seventeenth century house, "The Study", at Culross in Fifeshire. *Leonard & Marjorie Gayton*

Stonehaven, Kincardine: the curve of the harbour echoes and mimics the curve of the outer bay. *British Council*

The harbour at Pittenweem, a quaint Fifeshire fishing village, with a faint Cornish flavour.
Reece Winstone.

The harbour at Crail in Fifeshire has the charm of something in miniature, a toy. *British Council*

Dunottar Castle, not far from Stonehaven, is almost impregnably situated, and withstood a famous siege in the Civil Wars. *British Council*

St. Andrews in Fifeshire is famous not only for golf and its university, but for these ruins of its once splendid Cathedral. *British Council*

above: Aberdeen's fertile hinterland: a landscape near Rhynie, Aberdeenshire. *The Times*

Crathie Church, where the King worships when in residence at Balmoral. *Aberdeen Journals*

right: The Monastery at Dunfermline, Fifeshire, from the outside. *British Council*

Trawlers used in herring fishing at rest in the harbour at St. Monans. *Leonard & Marjorie Gayton*

Another view of the picturesque little harbour at Crail. *Leonard & Marjorie Gayton*

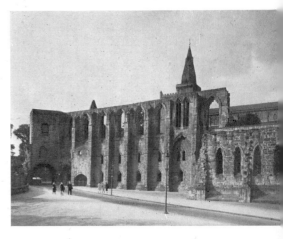

St. Machar's Cathedral, Old Aberdeen, with its twin towers, is one of the sturdiest looking of Scottish mediaeval buildings. *Aberdeen Journals*

Union Street, Aberdeen, one of the handsomest Scottish thoroughfares. Photography cannot show the clean glitter of the granite. *Aberdeen Journals*

Another typical fishing village street, this time in Auchmithie, in Forfarshire:
one-story whitewashed cottages. *Will F. Taylor*

A more northerly fishing village: the harbour of Port Gordon, in Banffshire. *E. W. Tattersall*

Herring trawlers in the Harbour of Fraserburgh, Aberdeenshire.

The valley of the River Dee, near Crathie, seen from the Banchory Road, Aberdeenshire. *Antony Brown*

Chapter 5

THE HIGHLANDS

"An eye," wrote Dr. Johnson gloomily, "accustomed to flowery pastures and waving harvests is astonished and repelled by this wide extent of hopeless sterility. The appearance is that of matter incapable of form or usefulness, dismissed by Nature from her care and disinherited of her favours, left in its original elemental state, or quickened only with one sullen power of useless vegetation." It is salutary to read these words after all the vague, declamatory, and sentimental passages that have been written about the Highlands. They were written, it is true, by a half-blind old man — "He does not now see me, nor I him," said Johnson at Baretti's trial — with almost no sensibility to natural beauty; but they are a fairly accurate description of some stretches of Highland scenery, particularly in Ross and Sutherland, in the far north, where the traveller may walk for miles over brown water-logged moorland, disturbed only by an occasional flock of mountain sheep, or by the wild cry of the curlew. Johnson is often thought of as an enemy to the Scots; he took a poor view of the Lowland Whigs, but he had a natural sympathy with the Highlander. Highland hospitality warmed his heart. He felt the qualities that the patriarchal Gael has in common with the Homeric Greek: "Without is the rough ocean and the rocky land, the beating billows and the howling storm; within is plenty and elegance, beauty and gaiety, the song and the dance. In Raasay, if I could have found an Ulysses, I had fancied a Phaeacia.' He even appreciated Gaelic music: "I have had my dinner", he says, "exhilarated by the bagpipe", and "exhilarated", for those who have a true feeling for reels and strathspeys, is just the right word. When he speaks of the cottages "which stood single on the naked ground", he gives a truer picture of these one-story buildings, thatched with turf, than travellers who merely note their picturesqueness, and not their wretchedness. He was also a stern critic of the policy of the Government of his day, which, by breaking the spirit of the clans, even before the great clearances had started, was already starting to depopulate the Highlands: "It affords a legislator little self-applause to consider that, where there was formerly an insurrection, there is now a wilderness".

If the north-eastern verge of the Highlands can be taken as Nairn, the southern gate is generally considered to be Stirling. From Stirling, by a series of deep glens, running roughly north-east and south-west, and by the valley of the Spey, the traveller can explore, as far as Inverness and rather north of it, a region of massive bulky hills, which, impressive as they are, are the worn-down stumps of once far loftier mountains. He will pass first through the rather self-consciously picturesque region of the Trossachs, adjoining Loch Lomond, with the mass of Ben Lomond, the southernmost of the great Highland hills, lying beyond it; in the Trossachs lies Loch Katrine, from which Glasgow Corporation draws its water supply, and which Sir Walter Scott made famous in "The Lady of the Lake." But this whole district, like everything with which Scott is connected, has a faint air of artificial romance and a more pronounced air of angling for the tourist. Moving northward from Callander by General Wade's famous road, the traveller passes on past more genuinely Highland scenery, like the beautiful valley of Glen Lyon, so rich in legends, and to the north again the valley in which Loch Tummel is linked by the Tummel river to Loch Rannoch, and across Loch Rannoch, Schiehallion, the maiden's point — a sharp conical quartz summit among many hills that are dull and round — presents a profile recalling some mountain in a Japanese painting. Following the course of the Tummel river, the traveller climbs between thick woods to the Pass of Killicrankie, where, in 1689, Viscount Dundee won his last battle, for a lost cause, and died; beyond that again, he passes the woods of Blair Atholl, climbs on for miles among bare moorland, until at length, through the Drumtochter Pass, he reaches the road that leads down through the Spey valley, and through the Eastern Grampian Mass, towards Inverness. On his right, lie the Cairngorms. Beyond Inverness, there lie three parallel Glens, Affric, Cannich, Strathfarrar, which each offer rough routes back again to the west. Beyond these, lies the bleak, barren, and on the whole uninteresting region of the farther north, leading, on the north east, to the agricultural plain of Caithness. Yet, monotonous on the whole as the far northern region is, there is a unique area, on the far north-west coast, between Loch Assynt and Loch Broom, in which sandstone mountains rise out of a bony landscape of almost naked gneiss: one of them, Suilven, a sculptured peak, which from one angle resembles a sugar-loaf — which is what its name means — from another, the back of a two-humped camel, is by general consent one of the most beautiful of Scottish hills. The Scottish hills tend, on the whole, to be most effective, when, as with Suilven and Schiehallion, their profiles rise in comparative isolation. The largest mountain mass in Scotland, that of the East Grampians and the Cairngorms, with their fairly level set of flattish ridges, often masked from the road by their foothills, does not offer profiles of such interest or beauty; but because of the hard igneous rock of which they are made, the East Grampians and the Cairngorms offer many climbs to tempt the hardy mountaineer.

These ancient hills, usually of volcanic origin, which give the Highland landscape its bony structure, have been worn down by glaciation, and at times submerged under the sea. They are scored with deep glens, varying from narrow clefts down which turbulent swift rivers force their way, to broader pastoral straths at a lower level. Along the course of these rivers, lie the beautiful lochs, often astonishingly deep; though some, owing to the attrition of the mountain sides, are gradually silting up. They are mostly lovely when, on a rare hour of windless and sunny weather, they reflect clearly their neighbouring mountains, and the firs of birches by their edge, and the clouds hanging above them; the small green islands, or 'inches', on these lochs, have a romantic air. In addition to the great lochs, there are hundreds of little lochans, which make flashing patterns, when the sun catches them, against the dark quilting of the moor. But the Highland landscape is perhaps most magical near the coast, where the scenery of mountain, valley, and loch merges with that of sharp tongues of sea, licking far inland; fiords, sea lochs, twisting kyles.

A Highland landscape, under a Mediterranean sky, would be astonishing; but colour is diluted, and the edge of things softened sometimes, by the misty and rainy atmosphere. Yet the rather dull, sodden grey and purple scene, which Landseer made familiar, is not necessarily typical. On a clear day, the light stippled green of the slim silver birches, the darkness of the firs, the bright red of the autumn bracken, the small, sudden flash of the little lochs, can give an effect almost of gaiety. But the changeableness of the scene is part of its magic. A loch, in which a whole landscape has been serenely reflected, can suddenly cloud and crumble to a cruel steel grey like an unlucky glass; the wind can lash it, the rain can pelt on it, till it churns with all the fury of a mimic sea. There are misty days when everything seem grey, or sodden brown, or gloomy purple; there are also moments at twilight when all colour seems scooped away and the distant outlines of hills or islands are picked out by a magic melting iridiscence. And all this, it must be said, is very general. Each glen, each district has its own peculiar combination of effects. It is only in the far north, in parts of Sutherland, and in the large flat coastal plain of Caithness, that the impression of magical variety yields to one of barren or fertile monotony. Caithness, indeed, is, with its fishing ports, Thurso and Wick,

Granite statues and
topiary, Fingask Castle.

with its well cultivated plain, more in tune with the Orkneys — which
are, in fact, a continuation of the Caithness plain — than with the rest
of the Highlands: Thurso and Wick are Norse names.

How do people live in the Highlands? Some facts about the Highlands

are too well known to be worth repeating, in anything but the most abrupt summary. The Highlanders lived under a patriarchal system, by hunting, by fishing, by blackmail levied on their Lowland neighbours: blackmail being, as Scott explains in "Waverley", "a sort of protection-money that

Lowcountry gentleman and heritors, lying near the Highlands, pay to some Highland chief, that he may neither do them harm himself, nor suffer it to be done to them by others; and if your cattle are stolen, you have only to send him word, and he will recover them; or it may be, he will drive away cows from some distant place, where he has a quarrel, and give them to you to make up your loss." During the Middle Ages, the Highlands could never be brought, like the Lowlands, under the feudal system; and during the Three Hundred Years' War with England, the Scottish Kings had always to be careful to guard their flank and rear against the Lord of the Isles, who was ever ready to intrigue with the English King. Scotland's great patriotic history is, on the whole, a Lowland story: and one of the greatest Scottish poets of the fifteenth century, Dunbar, whose work belongs to the brilliant reign of James IV, speaks of the Highlanders in much the same tone of humorous contempt that Shakespeare, in "Henry IV, Part I", reserves for the Welsh:

> Then cryit Mahoun for a Hieland padyane;
> Syne ran a fiend to fetch MacFadyen
> Far northward in a nook;
> Be he the coronach had done shout
> Erschemen so gadderit him about,
> In hell great room they took.
>
> Thae tarmegantis with tag and tatter
> Full loud in Ersche begouth to clatter
> And roup like raven and rook:
> The Devil sea deavit was wi' their yell,
> That in the deepest pit of hell
> He smoorit them with smoke.

The Highlanders, for their part, when they speak of the "Gall" (strangers) mean Lowlanders, and not merely Englishmen. They rose in 1745, not so much for Charles Stuart, as for their old way of life, increasingly threatened by the Whiggish Lowlands. At the beginning of the nineteenth century there came the infamous Clearances; their own hereditary lords, whom they had followed so loyally, turned them out of their wretched crofts. They drifted to Glasgow, to the new industrial belt in Scotland, or went overseas, to Australia, to Canada, where their record shows that there was no decadence in the stock. The sheep, with which it had been intended to replace them, did not prosper; and their inheritors in the Highlands became the red deer, the grouse, the golden eagle, and the yearly tenants of the shooting lodges. Attempts, like that of Lord Leverhulme, to bring them into the industrial system, have proved as futile as those of the great early Stewart Kings to bring them into the feudal system. They still continue to drain from the Highlands. There is nothing to keep the more adventurous young men; some local industries, like distilling and quarrying, but on no great scale; a little fishing, a little scrabbling of a wretched soil; employment on the great shooting estates, for a few permanently as gamekeepers, for more seasonally as ghillies; or work as a postman, a schoolmaster, a minister, a doctor, or running a general store (with bakeries from Glasgow, vegetables from England, and tinned foods from America) or catering for tourists. The Highlanders are like Red Indians on a great reserve, but less well looked after.

Yet they keep their pride, their warlike ardour, and the vigour of their speech. Scotland, as a whole, is only now beginning to become aware of the Gaelic tradition: to know that it is not a language of vague Ossianic maunderings, but has a bite in it, that can be felt in this fierce epigram of Mr Sorley Maclean's: "Though I am to-day against the breast of battle, not here my burden and extremity; not Rommel's guns and tanks, but that my darling should be crooked and a liar." The force of that in Gaelic verse can be imagined from its force in English prose. And their poetry, too, in Hugh McDiarmid's fine translations, supply reflects their seascapes, their landscapes: the fauna of these landscapes, "the little growling doe", for instance —

> watch her,
> Gallant, long-legged, swift-turning,
> Incalculable, her white-flared hips burning
> Like stars in the distance!

The great hope for the Highlands, as for Scotland in general, comes, I think, from the general cultural Renaissance which is now taking place. The Highlander, throughout history, has resisted change, because change did not offer him an atmosphere he could breathe in. The Lowlander, seeing, in the Scottish industrial belt, just where an undiluted Whiggishness has got him to, is beginning at least to understand the fierce, unyielding, and tragic attitude of the Highlander. The Highlander lives in a world of material decay, but also in a world of pride and poetry, of music, of ceremony, of noble hospitality; in manners, he has lessons to teach the rest of the Scots (it was of the Lowlander, not the Highlander, that Lord Rochester was thinking when he wrote, in his ode "Upon Nothing",

> French truth, Dutch prowess, British policy,
> Hibernian learning, Scotch civility,
> Spaniards' dispatch, Danes' wit, are mainly seen in thee.)

The Highlander will not be taught; but perhaps the Scottish tradition can at last become unified if the Lowlander approaches the Highlander determined not to teach, but to learn.

Highland dwelling places are less impressive than the Highland landscape. Typical of the larger town is Grantown-on-Spey, with its fine broad main street, and dignified classical buildings; less typical, but very delightful, is Inveraray, which, with its ornamental bridges and high, white arches reflects the expensive fancies of a late eighteenth-century Duke of Argyll; and there are ports to which decay lends a certain charm, like Ullapool, whose pleasant terraces, with palm-trees in some of the gardens, look down on a neglected wharf. Kinlochleven, in Northern Argyll, looks like some town from the Glasgow Industrial area transplanted, by black magic, into a circle of mountains; it was built by the British Aluminium Company to make use of local water power, and its working population came largely from the Clydeside. But most typical of the Highlands is the small crofting village, generally consisting of a single street of low whitewashed houses, a school, a general store, often combined with the post office, and several churches for different denominations, generally small, plain buildings, of a Georgian design, but with modestly Gothic windows. If the landscape is wild and savage, the settlements are human and subdued; and taken together they suggest a clue to the secret of the Highland character, its mixture of gentle melancholy and noble fierceness. That note, an echoing, an agonising note, is expressed, also, in one of the most famous of Scottish anonymous poems, "The Canadian Boat Song": the song of the exiles remembering, in sadness, the sad lot of their country:

> When the bold kindred, in the time long vanished,
> Conquered the soil and fortified the keep, —
> No seer foretold the children would be banished
> That a degenerate lord might boast his sheep.
>
> Come foreign rage — let Discord burst in slaughter!
> O then for clansmen true and stern claymore —
> The hearts that would have given their blood like water,
> Beat heavily beyond the Atlantic roar.

A fine view, showing sunbeams breaking through mist, of Stob-nan-Cabar, Glencoe. *Robert M. Adam*

Loch Long, from the "Brack" under a dreary and sombre sky. *Robert M. Adam*

above: A view of the Western Grampians
from Ben Lawers,
the highest of the Perthshire mountains.
Leonard & Marjorie Gayton

Looking southward towards Balquhidder,
where Rob Roy lies buried,
from the boulder-strewn head of Kirkton Glen
in Perthshire. *Leonard & Marjorie Gayton*

right: Four thousand feet high, the source of the Dee,
which runs into the sea to the south of Aberdeen.
R. L. Gerard

A view from the summit of Achallader
towards the southern aspect of Rannoch Moor,
fringing on the Black Mount. *Robert M. Adam*

Gleneagles Golf Course in Perthshire,
with a background of hills. *Balmain.*

left: The flat top of Ben Macdhui (4296 feet), looking west towards Braeriach ridge.
R. L. Gerard

Ben Nevis, the highest of British mountains (4406 feet) seen from Corpach across the peaceful waters of Loch Linnhe.
Donald McLeish

right: A beautiful snow picture, from the summit of Ben Nevis, showing the upper part of the Tower Ridge, a famous climb.
Dorien Leigh

The beautiful viaduct of the West Highland Railway at Glen Finnan, Invernessshire.
Will F. Taylor

Evening at Invercoe, Glencoe: white-washed cottages and black sombre mountains.
Humphrey & Vera Joel

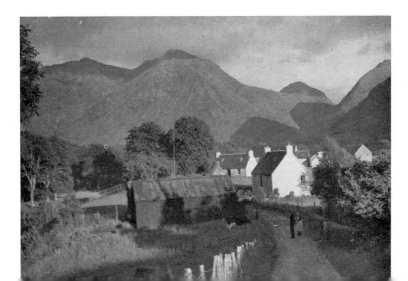

left: A magical scene of snow and tumultuous water in Glen Rosa in winter *E. W. Tattersall*

below: A typical scene on the North Coast, near Durness. *Will F. Taylor*

The Fair Maid's House in Perth, famous from Sir Walter Scott's novel. *E. W. Tattersall*

Inverary, Argyllshire, the most elegant of Highland towns. The church on which the avenue converges is an excellent example of Scottish Regency work. *Reece Winstone*

above: The snow-covered ridges
of the Cowal Hills, Argyll. *The Times*

Lonely against its sombre background,
the Kingshouse Inn, at Glencoe, Argyll.
Will F. Taylor

right: A quaint and charming
carved figure on a stone
in Kilmelfort
churchyard, Argyll. *Will F. Taylor*

A Highland graveyard at Kilmartin,
Argyll. *Will F. Taylor.*

Loch Lubnaig, Perthshire,
in a mood of reflective serenity.
Will F. Taylor.

Jean Macalpine's Inn, Aberfoyle,
Perthshire: a good example of the
primitive style of former
Highland cottage architecture.
Will F. Taylor.

above: Another view of Helmsdale, Caithness:
the harbour with the war memorial tower behind.
Will F. Taylor

Ben More Assynt, Loch Assynt, Sutherlandshire.
British Council.

left: Loch na Tuadh in West Sutherland,
with Ben Arcuil in the background.
A typical West Sutherland landscape:
bare rock, water and barren moor.
Robert M. Adam

The "sea gates of Western Ross",
looking towards Loch Torridon from near
Shieldaig; Ben Alligan to the left, Ben Liathach
to the right. *Balmain.*

A Highland flock on the road by Loch Shin,
Sutherland. *British Council*

A neat stackyard on a Sutherland farm, on the borders of Caithness. *Will F. Taylor*

Prince Charlie's monument, Loch Shiel, Inverness. *British Council*

A fairy island in a landscape of romance: Innis Shearaich, Port-in-Sherrich, Loch Awe. *Robert M. Adam*

Silver birches, (one of the most typical of Scottish trees) by the edge of Loch Assynt. *Will F. Taylor*

A little fresh-water loch full of boulders and water weeds: Lochan na Achlaise in Argyllshire, with the Black Mount behind it. *British Council.*

More silver birches framing a view of the River Garry in the Pass of Killicrankie, scene of Viscount Dundee's last battle and death. *Robert M. Adam*

Chapter 6

THE ISLANDS

From the lighthouse at Dunnet Head, which is the most northerly inhabited place on the Scottish mainland, you can catch a glimpse, across the racing seas, of a sandstone column which rises six hundred feet, sheer out of the water, a little to the north of Roray Head: the Old Man of Hoy. Such solitary stacks of rock are common on the coasts, particularly the west coasts, of the Orkneys, as are cliffs rising straight from the sea, and, where the violence of the water has in the end prevailed, great heaps of shattered rock upon the shore. The coasts, on the east as well as the west, are sharply indented with narrow inlets called "voes". Some of the smaller islands are mere rock and seaweed; others are given over to the pasturing of sheep; only about twenty of the whole set are inhabited, but the three larger ones, at least, Hoy, South Ronaldshay, and the island which geographers call Pomona and the Orcadians Mainland — between them, with their satellites, these three enclose the naval base of Scapa Flow — are surprisingly fertile; they resemble the agricultural plain of Caithness, of which geographically they are a continuation. Mr Edwin Muir, in "Scottish Journey", one of the most intelligent and sensitive of the books about Scotland to be published in the years between the wars, spoke often, indeed, of the prosperous, moderately sized, well-run farms of the Orkneys as presenting a pattern of life which industrial Scotland should admire; though it would be vain for industrial Scotland to think of following it. And if life in the Orkneys is more prosperous than the wild seas and the savage coast might suggest, it is also less bleak. The climate is comparatively mild, and summer, when, as in Norway, there is hardly anything that can properly be called night, but only a shining dusk, is peculiarly beautiful.

Kirkwall is a quiet, grey town, like Thurso or Wick, but there rises out of it, rather startlingly, an extremely fine Norman Cathedral. It was begun in 1137, and its history is peculiarly fascinating. At the beginning of the twelfth century, two cousins, Haakon, who was of a violent and jealous nature, and Magnus, who had a saintly wisdom and mildness, shared the government of Orkney. In 1115, Haakon got together a band against

Magnus and murdered him. Mr Maurice Lindsay has written a poem in which he envisages Magnus pleading with his cousin, not for the sake of his own life, but to save Haakon's soul: the "Orknetinga Saga" sets the scene. "Now it must be told of Earl Haakon that he summoned to him a large force and had eight warships, all well manned for instant action. And when the army was mustered, the Earl makes it known to them that he means so to settle up with Earl Magnus at their meeting that they would not both of them be rulers over the Orkneys thereafter . . . . Earl Magnus with his band of men arrived first in Egilsay. And when they espied Earl Haakon coming they saw that he had eight warships; then he knew for certain that there was foul play afoot." Mr Lindsay makes Magnus say:

> For me, this life is love, vaster than eye
> can fathom, wider than any ear can plan.
> My body is a vessel full of sorrow,
> your sorrows, and the grief of every man.
> And I have studied how a man should die,
> his praying heart hung in its proud, high place,
> the map of courage printed on his face.
>
> Therefore against your own best-bettered judgment
> hurt me, disrupt this body's ordered pose.
> I will accept, since only pure acceptance
> succours the dragging nails upon the cross.
> I will accept what pains are your betrayal
> to free the tight-wrung fabric of your soul
> before it tears on God's sharp testing shoal.
>
> If all my words have shrivelled in your rage,
> strike, and at least ensure time's infamy.

What Haakon ensured was Magnus's canonisation a few years after his death. Magnus 's nephew, Ronald, claimed his uncle's portion, vowing to build a cathedral in Magnus's honour if he made his claim good. St Magnus 's Cathedral is the result. "It is surprising," says Sir John Stirling Maxwell, "to find so magnificent a building in such an outlandish place, and to find it so full of French Norman influence and so rich in lovely detail . . . ." And, after describing various improvements carried out by Ronald's successors in the work, he goes on: "The result is a church of the first order rendered all the more impressive by the fact that it is the only large building in a bare and treeless country. The interior is equally striking. No one who has seen it ever forgets the first impression made by the length and height of its narrow vista."

The Orkneys, like the Shetlands, represent the vestiges in Scotland of Norse, not Celtic culture. Yet here, built around the image of the Orkneys, is a passage which represents as well as anything I know not Celtic Scotland but the romantic idea of Celtic Scotland: "What they sang was one of these Scottish lays, one of these ancient Bardic melodies, that are sung, even yet, beside the resounding echo of the Orkneys. In my mind, the words soared aloft, to melt, like the mists on the mountains of Ossian, suddenly away: like these mists which, taking shape from the foamy scum of Arven's torrents, thicken slowly, and seem to swell and spread, as, twisted and tormented by the winds, they mount up in an innumerable throng of ghosts. Here are the warriors, who are for ever dreaming, their helmets supported in their hands, and their tears and their blood falling drop by drop into the black rock pools; here are the beauties, pallid ones, whose hair streams out behind them, like the tail of a distant comet, melting into the damp bosom of the moon; they pass swiftly, and their feet vanish, involved in the vaporous folds of their white robes; they have no wings, yet they fly. They fly, holding their harps, they fly, their eyes cast down, and their mouths ajar with innocence. They utter a cry as they pass, and are lost, as they mount upwards, in the sweet light that summons them. Here are the airy ships, that seem to dash themselves against the shadowy banks, thence to plunge forward to the thickest wave; above them, as if to bewail them, the mountains bend forward, and the black hounds lift their uncouth heads and howl a long howl, gazing at the disc that shudders in the heavens; and all this while the sea shakes the white columns of the Orkneys, ranged side by side like the pipes of an immense organ, diffusing through Ocean a heart-rending harmony, repeated, a thousand times over, throughout the barracks that shuts in the waves." The passage is from Vigny: and this is the enlarged and shadowy profile of the Scottish past which Macpherson's "Ossian" projected upon the white screen of European ignorance. We tend to dismiss such writing, to-day, as vague, inflated, and fantastic. Yet this passage does evoke for me, very compulsively, a real vision of the rocky coasts of the Orkneys, a real sense of the loneliness of a moonlit night on these beaches with their untidy rock-stacks, and a real echo of the gallop and thunder of that far northern sea.

In their broken and rocky coasts, and the savage seas round them, the Shetlands resemble the Orkneys, but they are not so fertile, nor, though Lerwick, the capital, is a pleasant little town, is there any building to compare with St Magnus' Cathedral. The most interesting buildings are brochs, or round towers, remnants of the mysterious Pictish people, about whom so many intriguing theories have been concocted. Much of the land is coarse heath, which provides pasture for sheep and the curious dwarfish Shetland ponies. The people live by fishing and farming, and the women are famous for their knitting, as are the women of Faroe, or Fair Isle, between the Shetlands and the Orkneys, for their Fair Isle pattern jumpers and scarves. The most interesting thing about the Shetlanders is their dialect, a strong and craggy speech, showing strong Norse influences, in which they compose curious ballads, with refrains in yet another language, which is not any known language at all, though it is probably a corruption of Norse. Here, from one of their ballads, is an example of what I am talking about:

> Der lived a king into da aste,
> *Scowan ürla grün,*
> Der lived a lady in da wast.
> *Whar giorten han grün oarlac.*
>
> Dis king he has a huntin gaen,
> *Scowan ürla grün,*
> He's left his Lady Isabel alane.
> *Whar giorten han grün oarlac.*
>
> 'Oh, I wis ye'd never gaen away,
> *Scowan ürla grün.*
> For at your hame is dol an wae.
> *Whar giorten han grün oarlac.*
>
> 'For da King o Ferrie we his daert,
> *Scowan ürla grün,*
> Has pierced your lady to da hert.'
> *Whar giorten han grün oarlac.*

"Scowan ürla grün" may, or may not, mean, "Early green's the wood": "Whar giorten han grün oarlac" may, or may not, mean "Where the hart goes yearly." These refrains are handed down from generation to generation, by word of mouth, and the Shetlanders themselves are not sure what their meaning is. What does one feel about the other dialect? A little uncouth, like the speech of a comic Swede in an American film? Yet, with its mysterious refrain, this little ballad holds our attention; and it is with a pleasant shock of surprise, when we have read a little farther, that we realise that the "King o Ferrie" is gloomy Dis, that the King who lived "into da aste" is Orpheus, and that his Lady Isabel is Eurydice . . . . Unfortunately, like many once strongly rooted local things, this Shetland dialect is being ironed out by the radio, by newspapers, by modern education.

The Orkneys and the Shetlands were under Norse domination till the 15th Century. In the Outer Hebrides, Norse rule ended in 1266, and the people, though there is a strong Norse strain in them, speak Gaelic. The Outer Hebrides are a chain of islands, known collectively as the Long Island, and measuring from the Butt of Lewis in the north — by which Satan is supposed to have towed the island out to sea — to Barra Head in the south about 130 miles; the more southern islands are one of these enclaves of Catholicism in Gaelic Scotland which were left untouched by the Reformation. Harris has mountains, of grey glaciated gneiss, the ancient rock of which the whole group of islands is formed; but elsewhere the islands are flat and covered with bog and barren brown moorland, and without trees; and in the smaller, more southerly islands, in particular, conditions of life are extremely spartan. There is much to attract the naturalist, including many sorts of wild birds; but these are to be seen in even greater variety in the now uninhabited little island of St Kilda, which lies eighty miles to the west of the Butt of Lewis; it is the largest of a lonely group of about sixteen islets, and as well as its numberless sea-birds, it has some animal species which are unique to itself: the St Kilda wren, the St Kilda mouse, the St Kilda field mouse. Cruising steamers from Glasgow occasionally touch in at St Kilda, to give tourists a chance to see it. The general atmosphere of life in the Outer Hebrides is, quite naturally, rather bleak. But Stornoway, a herring-fishing port, the capital of Lewis, is quite a cheerful little town, with three hotels. The modern Lewis Castle, with its wooded policies, was presented to Stornoway by the famous Lord Leverhulme; and, like the town of Obbe, in Harris, which he rather foolishly rechristened Leverburgh, it is a monument to his attempt to reorganise the fishing industry of the Outer Hebrides on modern lines.

He bought Lewis in 1918, but got little support there for his efforts; undismayed, however, he then acquired Harris, where he seemed to be making more headway, when his death in 1925 brought all his schemes to a standstill. Obbe is a melancholy memorial to his ambitions. "The most enlightening view of Obbe," says Mr George Blake, "is got from the air; and from that angle it has an absurd aspect of something very up to date on the Merseyside or in the Thames Valley about Slough — neat rows of sheds and warehouses, trim blocks of dwelling houses, and cranes on

157

orderly quays — all on the verge of the fabled waters of the Minch, under towering desolate mountains, and in sight of Skye's fairy peaks of the Coolins." It is customary, I do not know why, for writers who could not themselves tolerate for more than a few days the primitive desolation os life in the Outer Hebrides to sneer at Lord Leverhulme's efforts. All hit calculations were humane and sensible ones; he disliked, as we all mus- dislike, the spectacle of social decay and of men extracting, from an un- rewarding soil, a merely marginal existence. But he was probably too simple and universal in his view of human nature, he supposed that the economic incentives that will work — with most people — in great industrial cities, would work in the Outer Hebrides. But he came up against a people who, by tradition, valued leisure and dignity more than money, who were not ashamed to seek help of each other when they needed it, who were inured to a spartan life, and who were not accustomed to compete with each other either for security, for position, or for money. These people had long, proud, and tragic memories, and their sense of being kin to each other, and of being unkin with outsiders, was stronger than their sense of individual self-interest. Economic planners must rely on this sense of individual and competitive self-interest, on motives of mutual fear and suspicion, and also on such worthier motives in each of us as a sense of shame at not making a proper contribution to the community, and a strong, if vague, sense of communal purpose. The unworthier motives were not present in the people of the Outer Hebrides, there was not the wish, which we feel in great cities, to be safe and anonymous, at the expense of much anonymous insecurity, but Lord Leverhulme, at least in Lewis, found it impossible to arouse the worthier motives either. He was, perhaps, too much of an outsider; without tact or breeding enough to arouse the enthusiasm of the subtle, ironical, and romantically snobbish Gaels. But no doubt he was feeling his way. In Harris, he seemed to be getting better results, and if he had lived he might have created something permanent. At any rate, he should be given credit for his good intentions; nor, because poverty, decay, and desolation lend themselves to picturesque writing, should literary travellers always presume that they are good things in themselves. What may have been a worthy motive, in the Hebridean resistance to Lord Leverhulme's schemes, was, perhaps, a dislike of work on the whole, as a servile thing, unless it is work on a man's own property — the barren croft, the battered old fishing boat — or work for some leader to whom a traditional loyalty is felt, or work that calls for some personal display of courage and skill; but admirable as all these motives are, when they lead, as on the whole they seem to lead in the modern world, to the decay of a community, they must be described as romantic. Yet romanticism can be a very powerful thing: on such intangibles, at least, this humane, capable, realistic man broke himself. The lesson of the story, perhaps, is that any future reorganisation of Gaelic society must come mainly from the impulse of the people themselves.

Skye is the richest, the most romantic, the most picturesque of Scottish islands. To summarise, in a paragraph, even in the most abrupt manner, its manifold attractions, is almost impossible. Yet Dr Johnson, who had the advantage of a lapidary style, and an eye too dulled to absorb detail, catches at least the weather: "Skye lies open on the west and north to a vast extent of ocean, and is cooled in summer by a perpetual ventilation, but by the same blast is kept warm in winter. Their weather is not pleasing. Half the year is deluged with rain. From the autumnal to the vernal equinox, a dry day is hardly known, except when the showers are suspended by a tempest. Under such skies can be expected no great exuberance of vegetation. Their winter overtakes their summer, and their harvest lies upon the ground, drenched with rain. The autumn struggles hard to produce some of our early fruits. I gathered gooseberries in September; but they were small, and the husk was thick. The winter is seldom such as puts a full stop to the growth of plants, or reduces the cattle to live wholly upon the surplusage of the summer. In the year seventy-one, they had a severe season, remembered by the name of the Black Spring, from which the island has not yet recovered. The snow lay long upon the ground, a calamity hardly known before."

Skye is a sprawl of peninsulas, sharply separated from each other by deep sea inlets. Its shores, except on the west coast, where there are great basaltic cliffs, are low and sloping. The roads twist round the heads of the sea lochs or cut across the bases of the promontories, following the coast. The low, thatched houses in the scattered crofting hamlets — the famous "black houses" — are exceedingly primitive, and as insanitary as they are picturesque. The scenery varies from barren, brown moorland to, in the Black Cuillins, the grandest range of mountains, and the most tempting to climbers, in the British Isles. These black basaltic hills are separated by the Sligachan valley from a range of lower, smoother hills, of crumbled-down granite, called the Red Hills; the rounded summits of the Red Hills contrast strikingly with the black, jagged ridges of the Cuillins. The Sligachan Inn, in the valley between the two ranges, is famous with all mountaineers. On the northern peninsula of Skye, which is called Trotternish, there is a very grotesque mass of heaped-up rocks, of all shapes and sizes, known as the Quiraing: they are composed of amygdaloidal trap, and the highest have names of their own — the Prison, the Needle, the Table. One of the most famous views in the island is that of the long green inland loch, Coruisk, hemmed in on three sides by the black and desolate Cuillins, and connected by a short stream with the sea inlet of Loch Scavaig. But to enumerate such items, in the style of a bad and breathless guide-book, is merely to confess the impossibility of giving, within a short compass, a proper impression of Skye. Much of the magic of the island, indeed, comes not only from its scenery, but from its associations. It was at the little capital of Portree, lying in the shelter of the isle of Raasay, that Flora MacDonald landed with Prince Charles Edward, disguised as her Irish maid, Betty Burke. It is rather sad to reflect that when she had him safe at Kingsburgh House, nine miles outside the town, he sat down to a hearty Highland meal, washed down with two bottles of ale and the best part of a bottle of brandy: "for," he said, "I have learned in my skulking to take a hearty dram." That Highland habit, in his years of exile in Rome, was to turn him into a wretched sot, make his young wife miserable, and throw her into the arms of Alfieri. But while his life was guttering miserably out, his legend remained, as it remains to this day, magical in Skye:

> Speed, bonnie boat, like a bird on the wing,
> Onward! the sailors cry.
> Carry the lad that is born to be King
> Over the sea to Skye.

Dr Johnson was not immune to that magic: and about Flora MacDonald, whom he met, with Boswell, at Kingsburgh House, he has two or three of these short sentences in which he gives, perhaps to an obvious reflection, an air of justice and finality: " . . . . we came to Kingsborough, a place distinguished by that name, because the king lodged here when he landed at Port Re. We were entertained with the usual hospitality by Mr. MacDonald, and his lady Flora MacDonald, a name that will be mentioned in history, and if courage and fidelity be virtues, mentioned with honour. She is a woman of middle stature, soft features, gentle manners, and elegant presence."

In the other sections of this little book, I have glided over obvious and glaring gaps in my accounts of places with the help of generalisations, perhaps plausible, perhaps merely facile; but it is impossible to generalise about islands; and there are so many more that I have not mentioned, small and large, dull and interesting, that I cannot think of enumerating and describing them all. The photographs, I hope, will do some of my work for me. I would like to write about Bute and Arran, where, when I was child, I spent so many holidays: but I fancy that my memories are neither history nor topography; they are merely memories of happiness. But there are two more small islands about which I must say something. Staffa is famous for its graceful basaltic pillars and for Fingal's Cave: Wordsworth writes about this, in his dull way,

> The pillared vestibule,
> Expanding yet precise, the roof embowed,
> Might seem designed to humble Man, when proud
> Of his best workmanship by plan and tool:

and Queen Victoria has a passage about it, in her diary, which is an admirable sample of her style of topographical writing — dignified, gracious, completely inexpressive of the places she is writing about, but beautifully and unconsciously expressive of herself: "It looked almost awful as we entered and the barge heaved up and down in the swell of the sea." But my last words must be about the little island of Iona, in which, in 563, the Irish monk Columba founded a monastery from which missionaries set out to convert the various tribes of Scotland. Our racial stocks are various; the temperaments of all of them are combative, and the geography of Scotland is far more suited to tribal wars than to unified administration; if Scotland has any unity at all, if there is such a thing as a Scottish tradition, a Scottish culture — yet I speak with hesitation, for all these propositions have been doubted — Columba is to be thanked for it. Only a universal religion, such as Christianity is, appealing to what is most nakedly human in men, could have welded into one society the Picts in the north, the Norsemen in the islands and along the coasts, the Gaelic invaders from Ireland, the Angles and the Britons in the south; and Scottish patriotism has always rested, rather more than the patriotism of some other countries, on a recognition of the common humanity, the common creaturely condition, of all men. For Iona, and for Columba and his work, as for so many other things in Scotland, Dr Johnson found the final words: "We were now treading that illustrious island, which was once the luminary of the Caledonian regions, whence savage clans and roving barbarians derived the benefits of knowledge, and the blessings of religion. To abstract the mind from all local emotion would be impossible, if it were endeavoured, and would be foolish, if it were possible. Whatever withdraws us from the power of our senses; whatever makes the past, the distant, or the future predominate over the present, advances us in the dignity of thinking beings. Far from me and from my friends be such frigid philosophy, as may conduct us indifferent and unmoved over any ground which has been dignified by wisdom, bravery, or virtue. That man is little to be envied, whose patriotism would not gain force upon the plain of Marathon, or whose piety would not grow warmer among the ruins of Iona."

The island coast near Sannox, Isle of Arran. *British Council*

Holy Island from the Arran coast. *A. K. Rittener*

Small boats in harbour at Stromness, in the Orkneys. *B. & N. Westwood*

Another view of Stromness. *B. & N. Westwood*

Lerwick Harbour, in the Shetlands. *B. & N. Westwood*

Seals basking on the rocks on the Shetland coast. *B. & N. Westwood*

Spriggie Beach, Shetland. Note the shape of the boats and the sheep cropping the salty grass. Fishing and farming flourish side by side. *B. & N. Westwood*

A view near Scalloway in the Shetlands. *B. & N. Westwood*

Shetland sheep being shipped to the Orkneys. *B. & N. Westwood.*

Women gutting herring at Lerwick in the Shetlands. *B. & N. Westwood*

left:
The G.P.O. cannot always be precise. Taken at Scalloway in the Shetlands.
B. & N. Westwood

Solidity of stone and wood: a corner of the harbour at Scalloway in the Shetlands.
B & N. Westwood

right:
A typical primitive turf thatched dwelling in South Harris in the Outer Hebrides.
Robert M. Adam

Drifters proceeding to sea from Castlebay, Barra.
Robert M. Adam

Wonderfully distorted basaltic cliffs
of the island of Staffa.
Those on the right,
curved like the sides of a ship,
form the entrance to the Clam-Shell Cave.
There are many caves on the island.
Donald Mc Leish

Thousands of black basaltic columns
support the roof of Fingal's Cave, Staffa.
The cave is 240 feet long
and the sea, even on the calmest day,
echoes within it like the boom of guns.
Donald Mc Leish

Barra Isles: view over Castlebay towards the south. *Robert M. Adam*

left: Tobermory, Isle of Mull: the site surrounding the bay. *Robert M. Adam*

Outer Isles: Uisgnaval More and Bealach a' Scal Pass, North Harris. *Robert M. Adam*

Stornoway Castle and Harbour in the Isle of Lewis. *Robert M. Adam*

right: Goat Fell, Isle of Arran: notice the typical bog-hole in the foreground. *A. K. Rittener*

Climbing among the Arran peaks— in the background Loch Ranza and Beinn Bharrain. *E. W. Tattersall*

Knoydart Hills and Loch Hourn viewed from Isle Ornsay, Skye. *Robert M. Adam*

The Isles of Eigg and Rum from North Morar. *Robert M. Adam*

Lewis township, Valtos, Loch Roag. Notice the low thatched dwellings and the dry-stone dykes. *Robert M. Adam*

Portree, the capital of Skye. *Robert M. Adam*

This Celtic Cross was brought from the isle of Iona to its present site in Inverary, at the head of Loch Fyne. *Reece Winstone*

High Corrie, Isle of Arran. *E. W. Tattersall*

INDEX OF PLACE NAMES

Illustrations are shown in italics, thus: *65*

First published in 1948 by PAUL ELEK PUBLISHERS LTD, 38 Hatton Garden, London E.C. 1

Catalogue 190/9   Printed and bound in the Netherlands

Jacket drawn by Barbara Jones   Layout and typography by Peter Ray, f.s.i.a.